MW00612644

"*Stewart's way of teaching is i
to follow. His information is ve
It makes sense.*"
Nadine M., Australia

"*I grew up in Hungary, without television and commercial
influences, and had many strange experiences. Everything
began to make sense once I found Stewart's website and
information. Now I feel I can put it all together.*"
Janos M., Hungary

"*I have researched many New Age modalities for years, but
Stewart's work is the first to truly bring forth my truth and help
me make sense of this illusion in which we all live. His work has
been a catalyst for the most positive and progressive changes
that I have ever experienced!*"
Lynn B., Idaho

"*After searching my whole life for truth, Stewart's work taught
me to look **inside** of myself to explain what is happening **outside**
of myself. I have never looked at anything in the same way since
finding his materials.*"
Celeste J., Illinois

"*It has been like a rebirth for me since I came in contact with
Stewart. I now see the big picture and work on myself through
all of his teachings.*"
Nina B., New York

"*Unlike most 'gurus and teachers' out there, Stewart doesn't tell
you the answers to your life's problems—he shows you that you
already have the answers and equips you for the search. He has
shown me that there is hope and we are all each others' hope!*"
Phil D., United Kingdom

Stewart Says...

By Stewart A. Swerdlow

Expansions Publishing Company, Inc.
P.O. Box 12, St. Joseph MI 49085 U.S.A.

STEWART SAYS...

Copyright © 2004 Expansions Publishing Company, Inc.

Cover, Typography, and Book Layout by L'OR Intuitives
Editor: Janet Swerdlow
Published by: Expansions Publishing Company, Inc.
                     P.O. Box 12
                     Saint Joseph MI 49085 U.S.A.
                     269-429-8615

ISBN 0-9740144-0-0

For further information contact Expansions Publishing Company, Inc.
P.O. Box 12, Saint Joseph MI 49085 U.S.A.
email: stewart@stewartswerdlow.com
       janet@janetswerdlow.com
Website address: www.stewartswerdlow.com

Other Books By Stewart Swerdlow

Blue Blood, True Blood: Conflict and Creation
Montauk: The Alien Connection
The Healer's Handbook: A Journey Into Hyperspace
The Hyperspace Helper: A User Friendly Guide
The White Owl Legends: An Archetypal Story of Creation

Forthcoming Books

Mind/Body Correlations
Thirteen Cubed: Case Studies in Mind-Control & Programming

DEDICATION

This book is dedicated to special people who have made my life so much easier and happier. Without their encouragement, support, and humor, much of my work on the East Coast of the USA would not happen.

I dedicate this book to my new sisters, Rosemary Muzek, whose song should lift the world to great heights, and whose cooking talents surpass any known chef in the universe, and Peggy Ann Schatz, (my P.A. System) who does call the shots, and is the universe's greatest organizer. Thank you both for all of your kindnesses, patience, generosity, hospitality, and graciousness. Thank you for being the true flowers in the Garden State.

I also dedicate this book to Evdokia Georgiou, whose incredible sponsorship, organization, and promotion has spread my work and seminars throughout the East Coast. She is an amazing worker in the fields of radionics, homeopathy, and harmonic resonance formulas. I have learned much from you.

I thank my God-gifted wife, Janet who puts up with all of my moods, idiosyncrasies and idiocies! I would be lost and miserable without her.

I would also like to thank my Oversoul, who allowed life experiences which I certainly could not have orchestrated myself, and enabled me to learn what I have written here.

Contents

*"You are part of the God-Mind and as such,
are a part of a vast and magnificent level of
consciousness that is known as the
Angelic Realm."*

Angels

Perhaps there is not a more misunderstood topic in the study of metaphysics than Angels. Almost every time that I speak to people about life and my system of understanding, the subject of Angels comes up. There are so many people out there "channeling" Archangel Michael, it is a wonder that he can do anything!

Angelic hierarchies are the basis used by the powers-that-be for a vast mind-control system using ELF (extra low frequencies) transmissions. Very often, programmers take valid spiritual concepts and Reptilianize them into a system that is used to manipulate people. The masses think that they are communicating with a higher power of benevolence, when in fact they are under a strong control system that skews their thoughts and beliefs in the opposite direction.

The Angelic frequency is part of your own Oversoul structure. This structure is part of you and can be tapped into at any time. This is who and what you are. There are nine distinct functions, or levels, within this frequency. Your needs and mind-patterns at any given moment determine what level is active for you.

There are no Angels "assigned" to you, but rather, your Angelic frequency level is active within your Oversoul structure at all times. Visualizing a silver infinity symbol over the crown chakra enhances the connection and awareness of this aspect of yourself. This can be done during meditations or visualizations. Keep a log of all of the information that you receive.

Keep in mind that Angels, which are really part of you, do not have names or designations. They are at too high of a level within the God-Mind to utilize such narrow restrictions as labeling. They are an energy. They have no actual form, i.e., glowing silvery-white beings with wings. Such images are conjured up by the brain to create a point of reference and an understanding of what is being perceived.

Take credit for who and what you are. You are part of the God-Mind and as such, are a part of a vast and magnificent level of consciousness that is known as the Angelic Realm.

"Pack up your worries in an old kit bag
and smile, smile, smile!"

Anger

You can only be angry at yourself. No matter what the issue is with another person, he/she merely reflects something from within yourself. You see only in others what exists inside of yourself. Whatever you are angry at in another, reflects an issue from within yourself.

Make a list of people who make you feel anger. Then under each of the names, make a sub-list of what it is about them that makes you angry. Take an honest look at the list to determine if these issues are really inside of yourself. When you do not want to admit that your anger issues are part of you, you project these issues onto others. You also provide a reflection for their anger issues as well.

This is true for any emotion or thought that you feel from another person, place, or thing. These are all simply tools that your soul-personality uses to see itself. The physical world is a mirror of the inner thoughts and emotions.

Whenever you feel anger rising within, stop whatever you are doing. Balance your T-Bar, or center a royal blue dot inside a royal blue circle at your pineal gland. Next, place yourself in ice-blue to calm your emotions and physical reactions. Once that is accomplished, put yourself in brown to ground and balance your energies. Then work on releasing exercises to remove the issues that reflect the anger for you. If you are conscientious and persistent with these procedures, you will no longer react with anger to trigger circumstances.

Anger looks bright red in an energy field. Old anger looks darker red or crimson. Anger is usually accompanied by frustration, violent behavior, high blood pressure, and/or digestion problems.

Anger ultimately leads to both physical and mental illness. It always results in relationship difficulties. Suppressed anger and frustration are one cause of cancer in the body. Is this what you want? Learn to tactfully and honestly verbalize your anger. Screaming, yelling, and cursing do not release issues, only enhance them. Speak softly but assertively.

You can think and feel anyway that you want, so why not think and feel happy, wonderful thoughts and emotions all of the time, in a real sense.

So, pack up your worries in an old kit bag and smile, smile, smile!

"Paint the picture of your life.
Write your story. Sculpt your dreams.
You are art!"

Art

I really do not know too much about art. I do not care for paintings that look like a monkey threw up on some canvass. I think art should say something to the viewer or percipient.

If you think about it, all of creation is art. It is the expression of the thoughts of the God-Mind. As co-creators, people do the same in this reality. Everything around you is an expression of your inner thoughts and emotions. Therefore, your life is art.

I really appreciate looking at a painting that looks like a photo of a scene. To me, this shows the efforts and talents of the artist who recreated a realistic scene on canvass. The same holds true of sculptors who produce a true-to-life image of a person that looks almost as if it could come alive before you. Michelangelo's Pieta is like that.

However, when an artist expresses anger or frustration, you might see a canvass splashed with swirls of red and orange. The image should immediately tell you what was in the mind of the creator.

Art should simultaneously tell a story inclusive of thought, action, emotion, and possibility. If you have to think about it for long, or walk away still confused, then it is not good artwork.

On the other hand, you may know what the piece tells you, and that may not at all be what the artist was thinking. That is okay. Art reflects the viewer as much as the creator of it. This is what makes it so fascinating.

Cities are works of art. They express the builders as well as the people who live in it. Your home is art since it reflects you. Even your babies are art—one of the most unique kinds that exist.

Everywhere you look, there is art. Every thought that you have is art. The hyperspace meaning of the letters for the word "art" mean: activation of creative balance.

Paint the picture of your life. Write your story. Sculpt your dreams. You are art!

"Most humans on Earth have had incarnations in past civilizations, including Atlantis."

Atlantis

This is a vast topic of volumes of books. I have written about it extensively in my books, and spoken about it in lectures and seminars. It seems as if on this planet, all roads lead back to Atlantis.

You can say that the island-continent-nation of Atlantis was the first human colonization on the Earth. All human civilization can be traced back to Atlantis, and from there to the star system, Lyrae.

The Atlanteans were not as nice as New Agers would have you believe. They were involved in the development of geomagnetic and laser weapons that were used to destroy rivals and keep others in line. They also had heinous genetic experimentation that created weird hybrid creatures that came to be known today as the Merfolk, Minotaurs, Bigfoot, Yeti, and even the domestic pig, which is half-human.

They were in constant war with the people of Lemuria who were Reptilians. The Atlanteans actually killed all of the dinosaurs in the world with electromagnetic and sonic pulses. They created races of slaves that did their field work and building.

The Atlantean language can be found within the words of Celtic, Gaelic, Cherokee, and other western European and American Indian languages. They were heavily involved with attempting to recreate the Lyraen civilization that was destroyed by the Draco Empire.

There were three main historic periods in Atlantean history. The first period was the colonization of that continent and the resultant wars between Atlantis and Lemuria. This was characterized by weapons development, and city building and rebuilding. A new type of culture emerged from the purely Lyraen refugees that originally came to the island.

The second period in Atlantean history was cultural development, global colonization, and scientific experimentation of all types. This was the longest period of time within the over 300, 000 years of Atlantean existence.

The final period was the one of destruction and cataclysm. This was characterized by the use of geothermal and geomagnetic devices that lead to the fracturing of the Earth's surface crusts which caused vast volcanic and seismic activities over many centuries. During this time period many of the Atlanteans foresaw the coming changes. Thus, many made preparations to either leave the planet or emigrate to different land masses.

Within the last destruction time period were three distinct epochs of continental break-ups. First, it broke into five large islands. Then some of these islands sank or broke up further. Finally, the entire rest of the landmass subsided into the ocean in one long day and night, leaving only the Caribbean Islands, Bermuda, the Azores, and the Canary Islands above the surface.

Many treasures, technologies, and artifacts remain to be discovered. There is a gigantic crystal still operating under the Atlantic Ocean that creates interdimensional openings from time to time. This area is now called the "Bermudas Triangle."

In the next 50 years, much of the Atlantean remnants will be discovered and revealed. The Illuminati already have gathered much of this material, keeping it secret over the past several centuries.

Most humans on Earth have had incarnations in past civilizations, including Atlantis. See what you can find out about it yourself.

"The Bible is not the Word of God.
It was written by humans and
altered many times."

The Bible

The Bible is a coded and symbolic work that is not to be taken literally. A few years ago, Israeli scientists working for the Mossad released information saying that the first five books of Moses are actually encoded texts that could only be deciphered by running the words without breaks between them through a computer system. In this way, sequences of letters which in Hebrew are also numbers, were found to contain entire messages related to the modern world and future.

The Bible code also showed potential futures and dates, stating that it was up to each person to determine which future they wanted to create. The implication was that all possibilities would occur somewhere in the vastness of existence and parallel realities within the God-Mind.

Interestingly, the codes were related to the cover story in the conventional part of the Bible. The computer was even able to show hyperspace archetypes encoded in the sequences of codes. When all of the archetype symbols were put together to create an overall master symbol, it showed a tetrahedron inside of an octahedron. All forms come from this one master God-Mind symbol.

In the past, as in the present, nations and cultures used words and statements from the Bible as a justification and excuse to kill other people. Most of the New Testament has been rewritten during Roman times to facilitate the goals of the Illuminati who then controlled the Vatican.

Every letter and word in the Hebrew Bible has a vibration along with the meaning. Studying this is a science called Gematria. By just changing a letter in a word, the vibration changes. By adding and subtracting vowels you can alter the meaning and manifestation. This is part of the Kabbala mystery which is understood in many Secret Societies. This is why the Illuminati love to play on words and meanings—giving them double and triple entendres.

The Bible is not the Word of God. It was written by humans and altered many times. The Old Testament was created by a computer, probably not of this Earth. Studying this code is a fascinating lifetime's work well worth the effort. Bible school will never be the same!

*"Children are the most marvelous things
in creation. Then they grow up..."*

Children

Children are the greatest blessing that anyone can have in his/her life. They bring you joy, laughter, and peace, even at times when you feel that you are at the lowest point in the universe.

Observing the pure innocence of a young child can make you realize how unimportant the rest of the world seems. Observing the expressions of happiness on a child's face from watching a bug or a blade of grass sway in the wind truly puts life's issues in perspective.

Observe the eyes of an infant as he/she scans his/her surroundings. Can you feel that way about your surroundings? Does chocolate taste the same now to you as it did when you were only three years old and just discovering its taste?

Any child that you bring into this world is attracted to your family by the mind-patterns of the parents. So, if you have wonderful thoughts before, during, and after conception, you will attract a child of like mind. Vice versa is also true.

People think that they must have enough money, or wait until the world is "safe," or they may think of other excuses to postpone having children. The truth is, whether you are ready or not to

21

have a child is inconsequential. The child will enter this physical world when *he/she* is ready.

Some people are afraid to have children because they do not want to recreate another version of themselves. They do not like themselves and fear another human being in the world who reflects that in their face all of the time. This is sad, because children change everything about you. You find emotions, ideas, and abilities that you never knew you had until you see that little face.

Some children decide that they need certain genetics for their bodies but do not want those physical parents to raise them. This is when adoption comes into play. Anyone can have a child, but not everyone can be a parent. I encourage you to adopt a child if you cannot physically have one, or if you have your own children but want to share your life with a less fortunate child. Any child that comes to you is by design and not by accident.

If you have many children, you will love all of them the same. You cannot love one child more than another. There are some children whose personalities you may prefer, or with whom you get along better. But you love them all the same, even if they say that they do not love you. This is like trying to telling a part of your own body that you love it less or more than another part— it is still all you.

Loving a child is the best way to understand and appreciate unconditional love. No matter what that child does, whether he/she is a scientist who saves the world, or a mass murderer, you will always love that child.

Be careful not to live vicariously through your children, as they have their own lives. You may not like the choices he/she makes, but you must encourage him/her to make his/her own choices— no matter what the choices. You can only gently guide him/her along. Keep a young child safe, but as he/she matures, you will see a new personality emerge that is independent and beautiful in its own way, and must be allowed to test his/her strengths.

Yes, children are the most marvelous things in creation. Then they grow up...

"Create your own rainbow.
Be a colorful person."

Colors

Colors are a major component of the Language of Hyperspace. I have written about it in my *Healer's Handbook: A Journey Into Hyperspace* (Sky Books, 1999), and have produced extensive videos on their meanings and applications.

I would advise everyone to learn and practice with colors and their combinations to see how they work for you. Humans are made up of colors. They comprise your chakra system. They are part of how God-Mind speaks and creates.

Not all colors are appropriate for physical reality. There are colors and shades of colors that do not exist on the Earth plane. Their vibrations do not fit into the narrow band of frequencies that exist here.

Humans love to see rainbows and flashes of colors in fireworks. This is a clue to your true energetic self. People are made up of colors that are the results of their vibrations, which in turn are the end products of your thoughts and mind-patterns.

What is your favorite color? What are your favorite color combinations? These questions provide you with information about your overall mind-patterns and general emotional status.

This can help when you do not want to analyze your actual thoughts and experiences.

For example, if you prefer pale blues, there are issues of depression and isolation possible. If reds are your favorites, then there are anger and frustration issues that should be released.

Some people dress all in black. This could mean that they are either very deep thinkers, or they are hiding something. Or both. It also means that they tend to pull energies from others and absorb a lot of information.

The meanings of colors are neither good nor bad. They just are. Do not judge them. Every color has both positive and negative traits. Your use of specific colors determine whether they are helpful or detrimental. Every color has a function somewhere in creation.

Learn the meanings and uses of all colors. Create your own rainbow. Be a colorful person.

*"Do not be afraid to say to others,
'Can we talk?' "*

Communication

Verbal and written communication are the lowest forms of communication that exist. Mental transmissions and intuitive reception are the most efficient manners of communicating.

I teach that the Language of Hyperspace using color, tone, and archetype/symbol as the communication method of God-Mind. This method is the most natural, involving instant thought understanding using pure mind and energy.

Modern devices like cell phones, televisions, computers, and pagers all receive and transmit electromagnetic energy and microwaves. As these pass through your body, particularly your head, cells are disrupted and altered. This is why cancer and brain tumors are so prevalent these days.

Using hyperspace techniques, one can open up the 90% of the brain capacity that is not used by humans. Imagine what powers and abilities you would have if you did this! Such capabilities as bilocation, levitation, astral projection, hyperspace travel, instant healing, time travel, and even immortality would be possible.

On the Earth plane, everyone needs to learn how to verbalize tactfully and honestly at all times, without waiting or holding back. The key words here are "tactfully" and "honestly." This means no yelling, screaming, or cursing. People think that when you yell, you let go or release. Wrong! Loud, angry verbalizations merely enhance the negativity, keeping it stirred up.

Remember, you are not responsible for the reactions of other people, only your own. If you speak up tactfully and honestly, you remain clear. If another person does not like your words, it is their problem, not yours.

If you do have trouble speaking up, then write your thoughts down first and read them. You might decide to change the words, but keep the content. If you have fear issues concerning confrontation, then use the following color code: first, place a layer of ice-blue around yourself to stimulate the verbal centers of the brain. This gives you the words to speak. Then, place a layer of maroon around that. This is the color of courage. These two layers give you the courage to say what you need to say. Use visual aids if necessary.

So, do not be afraid to say to others, "Can we talk?"

"Get out of the prison of your mind-patterns before you are thrown into a prison in this physical reality!"

Crime

Everyone knows the saying, "crime does not pay." This is the truth. It might seem to some criminals that they got away with something, and many of them do—in physical reality, but at some point in their existence, they will be called upon by their own Oversoul to balance the deed and compensate for their activities. In my opinion, once a person has committed a crime, it is better to pay for it while still in the body. When you wait until the body dies, then your mind-patterns project out energetic forms of your crime, and it will be a lot worse for you.

People commit crimes for many reasons: emotions, finances, anger, frustration, and even for love. Some are even called "crimes of passion." But a large proportion of crime is performed by mind-controlled, programmed individuals who are in an artificially-induced altered state. The original personality may not know when it commits a crime. There are even cases where people commit crimes while sleep-walking and the conscious mind is unaware of the activity.

Be that as it may, each individual must take responsibility for his/her crime since it was still within the range of the personality to do the action. Remember, programmers use what is already there and either enhance or diminish an aspect of the targeted

29

person. True, you might be artificially activated, but some part of the act was already within your being.

I was once activated to commit a financial crime. I had no conscious control over it and there were others acting as my handlers who manipulated me. I paid the price and went to prison. No one legally would listen to the real story. However, it was the best thing that ever happened to me. I learned who and what I was. I saw what was inside of myself. Even though I lost everything in my physical world, I gained the vastness of my Oversoul and God-Mind connections. I wish there had been an easier way for me, but this is what my soul-personality chose as the best way to communicate with me. The other people involved in manipulating and programming me will pay their price when it is their time. You do the crime, you do the time.

There are many of you out there who are programmed as sleepers to commit crimes when the trigger time is at hand. The programs are all based upon your own mind-patterns. Undo these, and you will undermine the programs. It is up to you. No one can do it for you. Time is of the essence!

Get out of the prison of your mind-patterns before you are thrown into a prison in this physical reality!

*"There are no "space brothers" sending
uplifting messages or warnings."*

Crop Circles

Crop circles are a seemingly mysterious topic that is really easy to understand. These shapes and designs that have gained popularity in recent years are mostly, if not all, man-made. No, it is not a pair of elderly English brothers who traipse the planet at night with wooden boards and rope making the circles or designs.

These crop circles, or what I prefer to call, "crap circles," have been seen for tens of thousands of years. The Earth is like a living being, which makes sense since it is a reflection of the mind-patterns of all who live on it.

Just as a human being has chakras with meridians emanating from them all over the body, the Earth has energy centers with ley lines crisscrossing all over and through the planet. This forms the Earth's morphogenetic grid. It looks just like a matrix with occasional energy balls in it.

When a hyperspace sentence of sequences, which is similar to DNA sentences, is injected into certain spots of the Earth, it replicates and spreads over the entire planet affecting the morphogenetic grid, changing and/or altering it. Doing this to the Earth is similar to giving a person an inoculation in the arm or buttocks.

31

Crop circles are attempts by those in control to alter the structure of physical life by entering new instructions or programs via the Earth's language, which is the Language of Hyperspace. The creation of crop circles leave traces of ELF and radiation in the structure of the field or crop. They are created via beams of microwave frequencies and electromagnetic pulses. This was done eons ago by the Atlanteans and Lemurians.

Crop circles were used at that time as a form "terrafication" or "planet forming" to suit special needs. This was later performed by alien groups who donated their DNA to create their own little projects, as a necessary physical support. Up until the 1980s, Brookhaven National Labs was the only scientific center capable of duplicating this technique. Now, crop circle formation is done regularly via satellite transmission and has become an Illuminati project. There are no "space brothers" sending uplifting messages or warnings.

Hoaxes are purposefully staged to discredit the real researchers. This also imprints the public with the idea that crop circles are all jokes not to be taken seriously. The media, particularly Hollywood, is excellent in perpetrating this dishonesty.

Many good researchers have been compromised, threatened into silence ,or into reversing their statements about crop circles. New Agers receive "channeled explanations" in regard to the meaning of crop circles. Do not believe these explanations.

"Know that your loved ones are in an energetic state."

Death

You are as dead now as you will ever be. Physical death is simply the transitioning from one form of existence to another. You do not grow wings and become an Angel the second you die. If you are a miserable person in life, then you will be a miserable person in the next existence as well. Learning continues. You take all of your attributes with you, no matter what they are.

All lifetimes are simultaneous in the Mind of God. Therefore, reincarnation is an illusion of a linear physical reality. In actuality, all of your existences are present in the Eternal Now. What humans perceive as death is nothing more than the non-physical environments that surround the simultaneous existences in the many physical realities. To the God-Mind, it is all one. Physical reality, being a mirror of the non-physical, is also an illusion. It is merely dense energy as compared to the non-physical.

Some people believe in a heaven and hell. I think that the life on Earth is really hell. The legend of hell, or Hades, comes from the stories about the Reptilians going to the Inner Earth, or deep underground in ancient times.

When a person passes on, they often go into the lower to mid-astral realms. This may look very physical and Earth-like, even though it is energetic for the most part with less dense energy. Here, you can meet loved ones who have passed on. You will also experience whatever you expect to experience. In other words, if you expect to see Gabriel at the Pearly Gates, that is what your mind will produce. This part of the astral level is like energetic clay that instantly manifests what your mind projects—both pleasant or horrible. If you think that you are going to hell, that is what you will most likely experience.

Eventually, most soul-personalities understand where they are and learn to go into hyperspace, which is pure mind and pure energy. This is sometimes called "knowing the face of God."

You have heard of the "white light" at death as well as the "tunnel." This is really a vortex that leads to higher astral levels or hyperspace. However, there is technology that can replicate an artificial white light to deceive and entrap soul-personalities when they leave the body. For this reason, it is better to go into the violet or gold light which bypasses all of the astral and leads directly into hyperspace. No technology can replicate this.

Human DNA is designed to live forever. You are immortal because the soul-personality is composed of God-Mind which is eternal. As above, so below. The DNA reflects this mind-pattern and creates a body that can live forever as well. It is the degradation of that mind-pattern that causes the body to age and get ill, or to have an accident.

The soul-personality obviously has an attachment to the physical body that it created. At death, when a body is preserved either via embalming, mummification, or cryogenics, then the attachment persists because the body is intact. The soul-personality cannot move on freely because it still has its body on Earth. This can be compared to being married yet separated and not divorced—you still cannot marry another person.

When a body is cremated or allowed to return to its elements, then the attachments are severed and the soul-personality can create another body if it wishes. Preserving a body indicates a mind-pattern of fear of death. The soul-personality needs to then learn that death is not an ending, but a continuation, of the Original Format.

While it is sad for the living to lose a loved one to death, the pain and suffering experienced is a living reacting to the death, not death itself. Know that your loved ones are in an energetic state. Since there is actually no space or time, they are closer to you than ever.

Exercise

Exercise is an important part of life. Since this reality is a physical world, physical bodies are subjected to physical rules and regulations. Physical bodies need to move, stretch, and train to last long in health.

You do not have to go crazy or be fanatic with exercise. Basically, everyone should strive to do weight-training three times per week, and aerobics four to six times per week. You should take one day off each week to completely rest the body. Every six months, you need to take a week off from weight-training. Then, when you go back, the body will build even more.

Females should weight-train as well, but not as heavily as males. Women should not have big muscles because this upsets their hormonal flows and disrupts their female organs. No one should take steroids. To look like a super bodybuilder is not a natural condition.

Men should have a good, well-shaped, defined muscular structure. Extremely large muscles are not necessary for men. Women should be toned and shapely, but not look like men.

Use weights that are easy for you lift ten times for three sets. Then, when you are comfortable with this level, women should maintain it, while men should gradually increase to more weight. Once men and women have reached their desired size, shape, and appearance, maintain that weight level. Weightlifting should only be done every other day. Your muscles need a day of rest in between to grow and maintain themselves. .

The same holds true for aerobic exercises. I recommend walking, swimming, stationery bicycling, stairstepping, skiing machines, rowing, and tae bo. Do not run, jog, or use a trampoline. These last three jolt the brain against the sheathing and skull bone, and can cause hematomas.

Aerobics should last for twenty to forty-five minutes per session. You can exercise aerobically on days that you weight-train. Weight-training is most effective when done prior to aerobic exercise. This is the most efficient use of your energy. Always wear comfortable clothing when exercising and exercise in a cool environment. Do not exercise in extreme heat, humidity, or intense sunlight. Also do not exercise in frigid conditions.

Yoga, tai chi, and chi gung are not physical exercises, they are energetic exercises. If you practice these, you must then expend the increased energy on a physical exercise, otherwise the body will burn up. That is why practitioners of these modalities look so thin and wiry, because their bodies have accelerated energies and are being consumed. While physical exercise is best, you can also do mental work like healing techniques, visualizations, and hyperspace work.

Do not be lazy. Take the time to exercise. There is no excuse not to exercise. Build exercise into your daily schedule, even if at first it seems difficult. After a while, you will find that exercise becomes a vital part of your life that is enjoyable.

Start your exercise program slowly. You do not have to be Mr. or

Ms. Universe the first week. Eat plenty of proteins and drink steam-distilled water. Take vitamins and herbs as necessary, keeping measurements to record your progress.

Remember to outpicture your "perfect" self before beginning, and visualize that self every day. Your body weight is not important. How you feel, look, and do is more important. The scale is relative. You can be a 200 pound fat man, or a 215 pound muscle man. You can wear a size 10 dress and look magnificent, or you can be a sickly size 3. Do not worry about numbers. They are meaningless when applied to reality.

Extraterrestrials

On the flow chart of existence the ET level is one step below that of Angels. This means that they are borderline physical and non-physical. They can be either at will for whatever suits their purposes.

By definition, an "alien" is a physical being that comes from a physical planet other than the Earth. An "ET" is a borderline physical/non-physical being who comes from any universe in creation, not necessarily this one.

ETs tend to be benevolent to humans, but will not interfere in the affairs of others. For this reason, they do not make themselves known. The ones who seek worship and identity among humans do not have human best interests in mind.

From this level of creation, humanity and other physical aliens came into being. Again, this level is part of your Oversoul and can be tapped into at any time. Very often, people think that they have spirit guides or ascended masters to whom they are speaking, when in actuality, it may very likely be just their own ET level of their Oversoul that is providing them with information.

Connecting to this level is merely a function of raising the level of energy vibration to a higher level. This is like turning up the power to a device, except your mind is the device.

Sometimes what people refer to as a "walk-in," typically defined as a "higher" entity that takes over a body and the original personality leaves, is really a "merger" with the ET level of your own Oversoul. This occurs when a non-physical aspect/personality of you blends in with the current personality to create a stronger "you." There is no need to change names or give up your life. A merger simply allows for a stronger, more highly evolved personality to exist by installing and blending a higher "self" awareness.

The ET level has its own civilization concepts, but is not attached too much to the physical. This level is more energetic and aware of the true connections to the God-Mind. Of course, that alone does not make them kinder or superior, only greater access to true knowledge.

While it is fun to tap into the ET level of reality, the ability to do so does not change why you are here on the Earth plane. Use the ET level as a reference as well as a source of guidance. But ultimately, you have total responsibility for your life decisions.

*"The most wonderful thing to do is
to unite the family of your own
personality aspects."*

Family

There are many groups of individuals that can be considered to be a family. There are families of plants, animals, insects, and even books. You do not have to be genetically related to be part of a family of "somethings" or "someones."

Some people do not like, or may even resent, their families into which they are born. They run away from the original family to start or join their own. Some say that they did not ask to be born into a particular family, but this is not true. Before you enter into the womb, you personally choose the best possible environment that provides the lessons and experiences that you need. You choose your birth family because this is something that only they can do. This is not always pleasant or happy, but it is always necessary.

Most people have close friends who often mean more to them than their own genetic family. These friends become your "family." Of course, you may feel that you want to replace your birth family with this new adopted family. That is an individual choice with mind-patterns behind these decisions. It is always best to attempt and make every effort to work things out with your birth family so that you do not recreate the same issues with any other family that you join or create.

It is also fine to have more than one family to which you belong. Not all of your families will get along with each other. They may not have anything in common other than you. Never force your various families to unite with each other. That could be big trouble. A common difficulty that many people face is trying to force your spouse's family to be friends with their genetic family. This will happen naturally over the course of time, if it is supposed to happen. Pushing the envelope results in hard feelings and fake niceties.

The most wonderful thing to do is to unite the family of your own personality aspects. You are very complex and made up of a family of alters. Work on making them all a big, happy family within yourself. After you do that, dealing with your outer family is a cinch!

"Eat well, live well."

Food

You are supposed to eat to live, not live to eat. People who desire food simply for the sake of eating do not realize that they use food to replace other types of comfort and security.

For example, if you eat when you are nervous and upset, you may subconsciously be remembering a time when your mother or caregiver plied you with food when you were upset as a small child. The mother or caregiver gave you food without addressing the underlying issue of why you were upset. This imprinting now propels you into eating when you are upset or depressed instead of dealing with the underlying issues.

Eating too much often makes you feel tired and sluggish. This in turn means you rest or sleep, so again you avoid your issues. If you gain weight, you get even more upset and eat more to dull that pain. What you really do is insulate yourself physically from the outside world. You put up a barrier between you and everyone else. Heavyset people also have thicker coatings from fat on their nerve endings. This makes them less reactive to outside stimulus which can be another reason to be upset and depressed.

I do not believe in diets. They do not work. I also do not believe in starvation. The human body is designed to eat on demand. When you are full, stop! Do not look at your watch and eat only because society says that it is time to do so. Eat when you are hungry and stop when you are not.

Eat food at a slow pace. When you eat quickly, there is a time lag between your brain telling your stomach that it is full, and the stomach sending a signal to the eyes to look for food. Chew your food completely and do not gulp, slurp, or gag.

Try not to drink too much fluid while you eat as this tends to fill the stomach before you finish eating. You should also eat foods that are as natural as possible, avoiding chemicals, preservatives, and anything artificial.

You need protein from animal sources. Vegetarianism is designed to weaken the body and mind so that you are more controllable. Human DNA requires the complex animal proteins derived from fish, chicken, turkey, and all types of red meats. Yes, vegetable protein is also needed, but it is not complex enough to sustain the human body for a long period of time. I have never seen a long-time vegetarian who is healthy-looking. They all look like a light breeze could blow them over.

I also believe that fasting for twenty-four hours, once per week is a good way to eliminate built-up toxins from the body. It is best to do this from mid-day to the next mid-day because psychologically you do not feel like you miss too much food.

Do not stuff yourself more before starting a fast as this only defeats the purpose. Fast on distilled water, possibly with lime or lemon juice; teas that are completely herbal and cleansing like green tea, ginger, hyssop, and chamomile; and/or noni juice.

Every three months, it is a good idea to do a three day fast. Whenever you break a fast, use light foods like cooked vegetables, soup or broth, or fruit juice. Take sea salt baths during the process as well.

If you flush any food or drink with violet color for at least 33 second before you consume it, that will clear out or neutralize any toxins or contaminants that may be in it. You should also mentally direct the atomic structure of the food and drink as you eat it so that it goes where *you* want it to go. Otherwise, the body/ cellular intelligence will store a lot of it as fat in case of starvation (Reptilian brain) and send the nutrients to places where it is not completely needed. You should also mentally thank God and Its energies for providing the sustenance with which to perfect your body.

Enjoy your food. Eat what you like, but try new things often. Food is the physical representation of what you mentally learn. If you eat a lot of junk food, you think that what you are learning is junky. Eat good food and it will show what you think of your life experiences.

Eat well, live well.

"You have got a friend in you."

Friends/Enemies

Whom do you consider an enemy and whom a friend? Enemies and friends are intimately related because they are both reflections of your own personality aspects and mind-patterns. Whatever you think of yourself and your relationship to the God-Mind within is the type of friend or enemy you will have.

There is a saying, "keep your friends close, and your enemies closer." Why? Because of the fear factor. If you keep your enemies very near to you, you can observe their every move and know their plans. But, if you know yourself, then this is already accomplished.

What is an enemy? An enemy is considered to be some person, or group of people, who have negative intentions toward you to one degree or another. So, figure out what you think your enemies are trying to do to or against you. Then you know what you think of yourself as well as understand your self-sabotage mind-patterns.

Once you make a list of enemy intentions, you know what type of release work you need to do. After you have made good headway in your efforts to release, you begin to realize that you no longer have enemies, but rather, friends.

Friends reflect all of the good aspects that you think you have within you. Whatever you like or love about your friends is how you feel about yourself as well. Your friends also reflect your feelings about your relationship to the God-Mind within because that is definitely your best friend.

There is another saying, "you are your own worst enemy." Conversely, you are also your own best friend. Which will you be?

Make a list of all of your friends, minor and major. Then make a list of all of your enemies, of all degrees. Include not only people but companies, government organizations, places, things, etc. See which list is longer. Add whatever intentions or feelings are associated with each one. Your next step is to release and assimilate the enemy side and merge it into the friend side. Watch how your life changes.

You have got a friend in you.

"Do not be the creation of others.
*Take control of **you**."*

Genetic Manipulation

In recent years, cloning and altering of the food on Earth have become widely discussed topics. Cloning was actually mastered by ancient alien civilizations like the Lyraens and Draco millions of years ago.

On Earth, both the Lemurians and the Atlanteans cloned and created vast numbers of hybrids for many reasons. After those cultures were destroyed, the art was lost for centuries and millennia, although the methodology and technology information was kept in Secret Fraternities for thousands of years.

In modern times, the Germans were the first to clone a human being in 1927. This was not publicized, but became part of Hitler's secret research in creating the perfect man. The Americans perfected the procedure with the help of German scientists allowed into this country under Project Paperclip. The first human clone in the US was created in 1967 at MIT in Boston.

Since then, the secret government has genetically manipulated corn, soy, and just about everything that they could get there hands on. They then created situations to enforce that farmers grow only this altered food. Anything else will not grow because the Earth is radionically treated to prevent the original seeds from germinating.

Inoculations that are given every year for the flu as well as to infants for immunities are filled with viruses that cause genetic changes. Viruses use your genetics to replicate, and alter your body as a side-effect. Many of these changes become permanent as the cells replicate from the new patterns. This is how all mutations occur.

Environmental factors like toxins, radiation, ELF, microwaves, etc., all create conditions within the body that allow these viruses to replicate and change you. The viruses themselves were created in the labs of Fort Detrick, Maryland and other locations. The viruses are released into the public via chemtrails, contaminated mosquitoes, or by actually spraying a community.

The goal is the creation of a new phase of humankind that meets the needs of the Illuminati and their goal of a new Intergalactic Empire, using Earth as its capitol. As you may know, genetics follow mind-patterns. Therefore, the body manifests whatever the mind-patterns dictate. So, in order to hold the enforced, artificial changes that the HAARP project and other programs induce, the mind-pattern must also be changed. This is why mind-control and programming are so vital to the New World Order.

The amazing combination of genetic manipulation and mind-control/programming is an ingenious and criminal duality that has forever altered humankind.

Perhaps this is the goal of the human species— to stretch God-Mind to incredible physical limits, defying the natural laws of this reality. Everyone has agreed to this, or no one would be here.

Remember—you are what you think. Who is doing your thinking? You? Someone or something else? What will you manifest? Why?

The choice is yours. Be what you choose to be. Do not be the creation of others. Take control of *you.*

"In actuality, the ultimate government is no government at all!"

Government

People seem to forget that in a so-called democratic society, the government, supposedly freely elected by the population, works for the people rather than the other way around.

These days everyone assumes that the government has supreme power over the citizens who must obey every rule and regulation that exists, even if it goes against previously established life-styles.

Somewhere along the lines there was a switch where now the people work for the government instead of vice versa. The government blatantly indicates that it does not owe any explanations for its actions. Everyone appears to accept this fact, appearing powerless and fearful to go against this sentiment. Like the guy said, "you are either with me, or against me!" There is no in-between, no free-thinking allowed.

There is now the admission of a "shadow" government that works behind the scenes to control everything. Years ago, many thought that this was a meritless "conspiracy" theory. Now, it is a known fact. Who and what is behind this secret government is not revealed, unless you read my books, of course.

For thousands of years there has been a secret global government that manipulates and controls the planet from behind the scenes. Now this knowledge is being thrust into public view. Because of the way it is being presented, the citizenship eagerly accepts this without explanation. The best slave is a slave who does not know he/she is a slave. This is a brilliant plan, but not a correct one.

Elections are a farce. The US presidential election in the year 2000 was a perfect example. This is when the American people learned that pressing the levers on their toilet bowls was more valuable than pressing the levers on the election voting machines. At least when you press the lever on your commode you know where it is being sent!

There is a world government in operation. Nations and districts are for public consumption and for ease of manipulation by the secret, now public, world government that promotes itself as the New World Order. This is a term used by Hitler and other zealous leaders who sought global domination under their control. The words "Novus Ordem Seclorum" are on the back of the American dollar bill. This means " New Secular Order" or New World Order. This is on the money…literally.

There is even an ancient pyramid on the back of the American dollar along with various other occult symbolisms. That is because the US is organized as a false nation with deceptive ideas and histories. Remember how the US was colonized and who set up the original government—Masons.

Personally, I am not opposed to a single, global government. This would help dissipate wars and nationalism that breeds violence and hatred. This would also make shifting finances and food easier from place to place. The Earth's population would enjoy equal opportunity no matter where anyone comes from on the planet.

I do have a problem with the way it is being created. The creation is part of an insidious plan that has been around for thousands of years. The plan is imposed forcefully and deceptively without regard for personal happiness or growth. This global government, which is under the control of the United Nations, is designed to enrich the few who are in control as well as consolidate their power.

True global government should be evolving naturally over the course of centuries. This is the natural outgrowth of nations that cooperate with one another as they work for common goals and uplifting of mutual populations.

I look forward to the day when the true idealistic concept of government comes into existence. In actuality, the ultimate government is no government at all! This is when people are so respectful of themselves and all others, that no overseeing is necessary; when governmental groups become optional and ordinary citizens take turns overseeing jurisdiction of projects for the good of all. Government then becomes voluntary and occasional. In effect, this is true Communism. Despite what history says, true Communism never existed. It was instead a form of totalitarianism, where Communistic ideas were mutilated, then militarily enforced against the people's will.

It is my prayer and hope that government returns to being of the people, for the people, and by the people. Not bye to the people.

*"Do not sweat the small stuff - all things
are insignificant in the vastness of
God-Mind."*

Happiness

You have all heard the axiom, "happiness is a state of mind." This is true because *everything* is a state of mind.

No matter what you feel right now, you can choose to be happy or sad. How you feel is a matter of choice. People, places, and things can stimulate you into feeling a certain way when a memory of a past event triggers an emotional response. But again, this is choice. When you decide that a certain experience was pleasant, you associate a similar experience with the original memory of feeling "happy."

The best gift that you can give yourself is to learn to be happy at all times, no matter what is going on around you. This is a special talent that requires sincerity and must not be forced.

Ask yourself what makes you feel unhappy. Make a list of all the things that fall into this category. Then ask yourself why these things make you unhappy. You might find that it all goes back to your childhood and that release work can eliminate these factors.

Take time every day to do or experience something that makes you feel happy *all* of the time. This can be as simple as exercising, eating a piece of chocolate, or listening to your favorite music. Once per week, or at least once per month, do something more special that makes you happy like going to a movie, eating at your favorite restaurant, or calling a special friend or relative who uplifts your mood.

Put things in perspective. Nothing happens that you cannot handle. Otherwise it would make no sense. Be happy about your life's experiences, because even though they may have been unpleasant and perhaps harsh, they brought you to a higher level of understanding and to a greater degree of happiness.

Smile, even when it seems difficult. Constantly say to yourself, "I am always happy, *now* and forever." Do not sweat the small stuff — all things are insignificant in the vastness of God-Mind.

Be *happy*!!!

*"The emotion of hate consumes a
tremendous amount of energy."*

Hate

You cannot hate anything or anyone but yourself. You may think that you hate a certain person, thing, or even a race of people, or a nation. But that only represents a part of you that you despise and want to eliminate.

The best thing to do is to make a list of the things that you hate about a person, place, or thing. Then, take an honest look at that list and ask yourself, "Which of these traits and characteristics do I have in me?" You may not want to admit that they exist within, so you project them onto others. This is often something that is hard to accept within yourself.

No one wants to admit to certain attributes that they consider to be hateful. Everyone possesses qualities and tendencies within that are not the best to have. Whenever you meet or encounter a person, place, or thing that reflects these qualities, there may be a part of you that "hates" what is in front of you because it activates that quality.

This is when it is important to start steps to eliminate the mind-pattern of that attribute. It takes linear time to do this. Be patient and do not rush it, or you will fool yourself into thinking that you have solved the problem very quickly.

Most hate groups are backed by government mind-control. However, these controlled persons in the groups must have hate issue already within for the programming to take hold. Programmers generally work with what is already there.

If you remember that absolutely ***everything*** that you see, feel, hear, taste, touch, or in any way perceive is a projection from within you and the species mind, and that ***all*** comes from the God-Mind, then it is ***not*** possible to even consider such a concept as hatred. You can only be critical of that which is inside of you. Everything is all God-Mind anyway.

By the way, hate is not the opposite of love; fear is! Fear is what induces a person to hate that which frightens him/her. Fear is about feeling separated from the God-Mind. When you realize that this is never possible, fear disappears along with hate. It is true that you may not "like" someone or something, but this is ***not*** hate.

The emotion of hate consumes a tremendous amount of energy, causing stress to accumulate. This, in turn, creates illness in the body. This is not desirable. Do not hate.

"Your health, or lack of it, is a direct result of your thoughts."

Health/Illness

These are actually the same thing…the status of the current mind-pattern. What you think is what you become. The mind produces the physical effects based upon the electromagnetic qualities of thought. These qualities can be observed as the product of what the thought creates.

Everyone is given a chance to correct a mind-pattern. When you do not, the negative thought degenerates into an emotional condition. If you do not correct it then, it becomes a physical manifestation as an illness in the body or mind, depending upon the projection.

Each part of the body represents a thought, or a thought-band, that coalesces into an energy center. Whenever you have an illness, you can determine the mind-pattern from the part of the body that is affected. For example, the legs and feet represent stepping into the future as well as the future support structure. When you are worried or concerned about the future, the legs and feet manifest a problem symbolic of that.

When you have deep emotional issues that you do not release, the heart and lungs are affected. When you do not feel supported in life, the spinal column suffers, and so on with other sections of

61

the body, based on the specific belief that you hold.

When you do the basics of chakra spinning, T-Bar balancing, breathing, and release work, the body responds with health, energy, and vitality. The DNA in your body is designed to last indefinitely, and is stronger than any computer chip. Humans are designed to live forever. The only thing that causes aging, illness, and death is the thought of such things.

You can mentally convert anything that you eat or drink into creative tissues for the body. All of this is discussed in my *Healer's Handbook* and my *Triad Healing* videos. Always think positive thoughts. Whenever you catch yourself thinking negatively, put a big, brown "X" through the thought and replace it with a reverse, positive thought. As you become more proficient with this the process become second nature.

You can think any thought that you wish. Why would you want to think something that harms your body? There is a saying, "the body does not lie." This means that you are a living statement of all of your self-beliefs. The body is constructed by the blueprint of your DNA. Your DNA is created by atomic structure forming around the electromagnetic energies of your thought streams or mind-patterns. Literally, you are what you think!

Your health, or lack of it, is a direct result of your thoughts. You must take responsibility for yourself. The environment, accidents, germs, and toxins are tools that the mind uses to create dis-ease. Think happy, peaceful, healthy thoughts!

*"Learn the truth of where you came from
as well as who and what you truly are."*

History

Almost everything you know about history is a lie. Most of it is rewritten or fabricated to promote Illuminati views of the world and provide you with "proof" of historical facts.

Most countries are a creation of the various Illuminati families to strengthen their positions with local inhabitants. Borders and boundaries were arbitrarily and strategically drawn.

Countries like Switzerland, Kuwait, Yugoslavia, Israel, and even the United States of America, are all artificially created. In fact, the USA is actually the Virginia Corporation based in London. You can look up more of this data on my website and books.

Many of the figures from ancient history were also fabricated. Sometimes, a group of them were conglomerated into a single superhero. Conversely, many mythical figures were actually real personages who were relegated to mythical status so that they would have no real value to those who learned about them.

The founding fathers of the Unites States were mostly Masons and Illuminati lackeys who created a front for their European masters. They killed the native peoples so that the colonists could not learn about secret ways to access the God-Mind.

Europe was first colonized by Atlantean refugees and then conquered by the hybrid descendents from Sumeria who also controlled ancient Egypt and India. Most western Jews are actually descendents of the Hazards from the Caucasus Mountains who entered into Europe after converting en masse to Judaism in the 800s AD. They did this to avoid control by Rome.

There is much more to tell, but that is not the purpose of this book. Read my book, *Blue Blood, True Blood: Conflict & Creation* (Expansions Publishing, 2002) for true history. Everything that you learned in school was based on lies and deception. The same is true for science, philosophy, and religion.

Do not be a mindless robot. Learn the truth of where you came from as well as who and what you truly are. Do your own research and pass the truth on to keep future historical accounts accurate.

"Never side with any parent against your spouse. Never side with your spouse against any parent."

In-Laws

What a topic! Do you have in-laws or out-laws? In all honesty, I think that the manifestation of problems stems more from them than from you. Even though you are reflections of each other, my experience has been in my years of counseling that it is usually the in-laws who initiate the need to control and manipulate. It is up to you how you respond to that.

Mothers rarely believe that their children marry a spouse that is good enough for them. Mothers usually have issues with son-in-laws and daughter-in-laws. Fathers generally tolerate, and sometimes get along with, daughter-in-laws, but not as often as a son-in-laws.

What is going on here? Since most people tend to marry versions of their own parents, you usually first compare your spouse to your spouse's parents. Then, you compare your parents to your in-laws. Because the parents want only the best for their child, a conflict develops when the child marries someone who does not meet the parents' standards. Such parents tend to be over-protective, manipulating, and difficult to please. They often do not get along with their own spouse, parents, or in-laws.

What to do? The best thing is release work on your own parents.

Speak to your spouse about how you feel about your in-laws and discuss ways to mutually deal with certain behaviors and attitudes. Never side with any parent against your spouse. Never side with your spouse against any parent. Never side with your child against a spouse, unless the spouse is abusive and the child is in danger.

If either set of parents becomes too difficult and they interfere in your personal lives, then **both** husband and wife must *tactfully* confront the parents to explain their feelings and discuss changes. If change is not forthcoming, then limit the amount of time spent with them. *Never* use grandchildren as a weapon.

Remember, if someone causes problems in your life, you must honestly decipher that person's reflection of yourself. There is some trait or characteristic projected from within that your in-law only reflects back to you. Make every effort to figure out what that is so that you can work on *yourself*! Then the problem dissipates.

Do not yell, scream, or mutter under your breath. They can hear you. They will use it against you and bring it up "'til Kingdom come." Look at it as a way of clearing out "stuff" within yourself. In the end, it will all be worth it.

I am blessed with wonderful in-laws...so are you.

"There is a reason it is called the Worldwide Web. Spiders make webs to entrap their prey."

The Internet

Although the Internet is completely about mind-control and unifying global information, this is perhaps one of the greatest inventions to date. The Internet is convenient, easy, and literally puts the entire planet at your disposal.

I realize that every keystroke is monitored and "they" always know what you are up to, but it is a wonderful way of communicating and finding information about absolutely anything.

Eventually, your brain will operate similar to the Internet. This will be accomplished internally with a brain implant. Then, as a cyber, all you have to do is think of something or someone, and you will connect with them through the implant within your brain. This will eliminate the need for cell phones, computers, fax machines, etc. Images will be instantly downloaded into the brain and stored there for use.

This also means that every thought and emotion will also be instantly transmitted to a central monitoring computer that will determine if you are a threat to the NWO and in need of "re-education." Basically, at that point, there will be absolutely no personal freedom, even within your own mind.

There is a reason it is called the Worldwide Web. Spiders make webs to entrap their prey. You can figure out the analogy yourself.

Still, I think that you can use what is there to your advantage. Learn all that you can about whatever subjects interest you. Communicate with people and organizations of like mind. Write articles and stories that release your mind-patterns.

Remember, the outer reflects the inner. Therefore, the Internet symbolizes the connections that each person has to his/her alternate selves, your soul-personality's simultaneous existences, your Oversoul, and to the real central computer – the God-Mind within.

Do visualizations of the "computer of the mind" to establish the awareness of this. Everything is already within, you just have to use it. Keep a log of what you discover. The Internet of the outside world will become the Internal-Net of your Oversoul/ God-Mind.

You will probably never get through the entire Internet in one lifetime. You certainly have all of eternity to look at your own Internal-Net. So, sign on! You have mail!

"The legal system is a giant clique."

Legal Profession

Somewhere in the vastness of Biblical literature is a passage that reads, "woe unto thee lawyer, for thou removes the key to knowledge."

Everything in Western society, and particularly in the US, revolves around legal matters with thick, non-comprehensible contracts. You cannot get married, divorced, incorporated, make a deal, die, or buy anything, without a legal document.

Most politicians are lawyers. That says a whole lot. The entire world is run from a legal control system from the United Nations down to the local family-owned grocery. There is not one aspect of life that is not dominated by some legal code.

No one that I know of can really understand the gobble-de-gook that is in every legal paper. Contracts and laws are written in such a way as to confuse and repel any non-lawyer who researches it. In this way, lawyers retain power over the population because no one can understand what is written. Then, the lawyer becomes indispensable since he/she is the only one who can understand and translate the documents.

One must also question the motives of a person who defends a heinous criminal. Why would anyone defend the rights of a person who raped children, killed indiscriminately, or participated in war crimes? The answer is money. In this respect, lawyers are even worse than doctors. Lawyers will do anything for money, even when they know that their client is clearly wrong.

Lawyers do not care about your feelings. They care only about their fee and if you have the money to pay them. If you do not have money, than your case better be one of fame or in the limelight so the lawyer can get publicity.

Yes, there are some lawyers who work for justice and righting wrongs. They are extremely rare and not doing well financially. Most of them wind up writing books and making money that way.

The legal system is a giant clique. Lawyers, prosecutors, judges, and the police work together to condemn a person even before a trial begins. The deal is done before the jury is selected. That is the American way. There is a gold fringe on court flags for a reason!

Yes, woe unto thee lawyer—for you will meet *your* judgement when your days on Earth are through!

*"Much of Lemuria remains to
be discovered."*

Lemuria

Of course no tale of Atlantis is complete without a discussion of Lemuria. This ancient continent was the location of the first colonists on the Earth, who were Reptilians. They arrived from the Draco star system in an object/vehicle that is now known as the Moon.

The Reptilians were androgynous beings with a society based on the military and caste systems. They occupied a large, mountainous and volcanic island in what is today known as the Pacific Ocean. This island-continent was destroyed during a war with Atlantis during which the Atlanteans harnessed the geomagnetic forces of the Earth to fracture the tectonic plates under Lemuria, in turn causing it to subside into the water.

Remnants of this continent are Japan, Taiwan, The Philippines, Indonesia, Australia, New Zealand, Hawaii, all the South Pacific islands, and California west of the San Andreas fault line. Parts of Lemuria still rise and fall in the southeastern Pacific between New Zealand and Chile.

When Lemuria sank, the survivors fled to the inner Earth via the tunnel and tube system that exists in the Earth's upper crust. Thus began the legends of hell and demons that live under the Earth.

The Lemurians eventually began a hybridization program that led to the development of the current Illuminati. In effect, the Lemurian/Draco culture never left the Earth. Their culture is the oldest civilization on the Earth.

The ancient war between the two superpowers is documented in the ancient Indian Vedas where flying ships called Vimanas and missile-like weapons are described. These texts are over 100,000 years old at the least.

The story of Adam and Eve is an allegorical description of the separation of an androgynous Reptilian body into male and female components. Human genetics were added to a base Reptilian body. This is why in the womb, a fetus looks first Reptilian with the development of human features following. DNA opens in the sequence in which it was built.

Much of Lemuria remains to be discovered. There is a counterpart to the Atlantic Ocean's Bermuda Triangle in the Pacific Ocean called the Devil's Triangle. The Devil's Triangle is in the Pacific Ocean bordered by southern Japan, Guam, and The Philippines. The Devil's Triangle is directly opposite the Bermuda Triangle. These are massive energy points on the Earth's grid into which artificially created crystals were placed to tap into the morphogenetic grid of the Earth to enhance and utilize its geomagnetic powers.

In the 21st century, many artifacts and some information concerning Lemuria will be revealed to the public by the Illuminati. This information will be skewered and altered to make the old land look like it was a paradise filled with benevolent beings from who the Illuminati is descended—this is an understandable slant.

There is now a second moon in orbit filled with Draco warriors. These warriors have come to join with their Lemurian/Inner Earth descendents in order to assimilate this planet into their

Empire. This may cause trouble for the Illuminati. This will all be quite an interesting show!

*"True love is unconditional, deep,
eternal, and goes beyond any
physical words."*

Love

Most people consider love to be an emotion as well as the greatest power in the universe. Love is all of this, but also something else. Love is merely one of the 12 energies that emanate from the God-Mind that passes through the 10 aspects of God-Mind, forming a matrix.

Love is mostly neutral, as are all of the 12 energies. They come into action when mind directs them. Love is a tool that is to be used. By itself, it is inert. For example, I can take a knife and carve a beautiful statue. Or, I could kill you with it. The knife itself does nothing—what the knife does depends upon how the user manipulates it. In the same way, I can love you unconditionally, or I can love you to death. This is still the same energy, but put to different uses.

This is why I am continually amused by people coming up to me after a lecture and asking, "Can't we just send love to the Illuminati so they will change or go away?" Nice thought, but it does not work that way. You can send love to anyone or anything you want, but that does not mean they have to accept it!

You cannot impose love on another, nor can you buy it. A child will "love" **anyone** who buys him/her a toy or favorite candy.

That lasts about five minutes and is not unconditional. True, unconditional love lasts forever. If you "love" someone as long as they act a certain way, that is **not** love. If you really love another, no matter what they do, even to you, you still love them. You may not like them or their actions, but you still love them. Anyone who ever had a child knows this. That child could call you names and stab you in the heart, and you will love them. That is unconditional love.

When a couple divorces with bitter, nasty arguments, this is a sign that they still love each other. Otherwise, they would not care what the other one says or thinks. You always hurt the one you love. Why? Because that may be the only way you can get any attention from them. Even if it is only negative attention. That is why children, and some adult men, throw temper tantrums.

Usually, men associate or think that love has to do with beauty or desire. Women think that love is caring and dedication. This is only a small part of love. True love is unconditional, deep, eternal, and goes beyond any physical words. True love is not something that you find because it is **always** inside of you, like all God-Mind energies. You just have to use it. Apply it to everyone and everything in your life. See what happens!

*"Physician, heal thyself! Go to the cause,
not the symptom. Heal, instead of mask.
Cure, instead of remove. Do no harm."*

Medical Profession

Most of you already know how I feel about the medical profession. Today's medical profession exists for profit only, not for patient care. Many doctors are considering (or have already done so) leaving their profession since insurance no longer pays for treatment the same way as it did years ago.

I have a client who is a teacher in a medical school in the US. This person told me that the joke in medical school is, " Hurry up and operate before the patient gets better." Not a very funny joke.

The sad truth is that doctors are taught to spend less than ten minutes with each patient to be as money-efficient as possible. The longer time spent with a patient, the less they earn.

My own mother-in-law went to a cardiologist after her heart surgery. She had a list of questions for him because she was concerned about her medications and the way she was feeling. After listening to a few of her queries, he said, "You ask too many questions," and walked out of the room! If he had done that to me, he would be eating his stethoscope!

Most physicians refuse to even consider alternative herbs, vitamins, or non-conventional therapies, even though they have been proven over the centuries to be valid. If it is not in a medical journal, they will not pay attention.

Doctors particularly love to pluck out organs that are not needed for daily use. They do this especially with women. There is hardly a woman over fifty that has not been asked to remove her ovaries, uterus, thyroid, gall bladder, or breast. Pretty soon, there will be a lot of hollow women walking around!

Psychiatrists love to put people on drugs. The side-effects are more horrendous than the mental condition, but they will say you are better. They even invent social disorders in order to drug you. The same goes for children—how many do you know who are on Ritalin or other mind-numbing medications?

Physician, heal thyself! Go to the cause, not the symptom. Heal, instead of mask. Cure, instead of remove. Do no harm. That is part of the oath that is taken. They are not listening—they are busy calling their stockbrokers.

*"Your health, sleep, and moods are
always so much better when you
meditate regularly."*

Meditation

Meditation is a function of the right-brain. Meditation occurs when you listen to the God-Mind within you. Very often, it is during meditation that you receive an answer to the prayer of the left-brain. The answer may come as a flash of intuition, a symbol, a word or number, a color or tone, or even as a movie-like image.

If possible, it is a good idea to meditate once or twice per day when you have quiet time for about ten to twenty minutes. Meditation acts to reset your thought structure as well as clear your mind of clutter and junk.

All that you need to do is sit or lie down in a comfortable and quiet place at a time when you know that you will not be interrupted. Balance your T-Bar, and do a few cleansing breaths. Breathe in slowly through the nostrils, hold for a few moments, then slowly blow out through the mouth. There are many variations on breathing before meditating. Concentrating on breathing solely through the left nostril activates the right hemisphere of the brain and enhances the meditative state.

Then, center your consciousness at the pineal gland in royal blue, and slowly move the consciousness into the right hemisphere.

Just wait and observe. Do nothing else. When you are ready to leave this state, center back at the pineal gland and do a couple more breaths. When you are done, put yourself in brown to ground and balance your energy.

If you are looking for a specific answer to a specific challenge, then use some type of visual at the pineal gland as a focal point. Then, move the consciousness into the right hemisphere. Whatever you receive will be related to this image.

Some people find it mood-enhancing to use soft music, incense, colored lights, etc. to do their meditations. I find them to be distractions because you might focus on them instead of the right-brain. Certain smells and sounds do activate the right-brain, so they can be helpful. This depends upon your own ability to concentrate.

Never do group or global meditations as these can become targets for ELF. You might also pick up "stuff" from others—it is best to work alone when meditating.

Your health, sleep, and moods are always so much better when you meditate regularly.

*"When you do not take responsibility for
your actions or life, then you allow another
force to take control of you."*

Mind-Control
& Programming

Wow! There is a lot to say about the massive topic of mind-control and programming. I have videos on this subject in great detail. So, I will just tell you my feeling about this.

The entire world is mind-controlled and programmed to one degree or another. Everyone is like a puppet or robot who awaits the signals from the masters and controllers. When they issue a certain trigger, everyone jumps this way or that. Not having your own mind, or control of your mind, means that you act out whatever they have preprogrammed into you.

Ultimately, people will become what is depicted on the newer Star Trek shows, similar to the alien race called "The Borg." These are part organic, part computerized cyborgs all connected to a central computer that is referred to as "The Collective." In this scenario, no one has an individual thought. All act as one. It is a mass consciousness that is an artificial species group mind.

There are ways to deprogram from this. This takes time and effort, and may not happen within the span of your current lifetime. But, you must start someplace.

Do not blame the Illuminati for your programming.

Programming is only possible because of your victimization mentality that attracted the controllers. You have a choice on this planet. Either you control your own mind, or someone else will control it for you. There is no better place in the entire galaxy for you to overcome this mind-pattern.

Your brain is like a computer, interacting with others in a manner that reflects the "software" of the mind. The brain is a device that the mind uses. The software is the mind-pattern that directs the brain. When you do not take responsibility for your actions or life, then you allow another force to take control of you. This makes you feel that you are relieved of responsibility. However, this is not true. The desire to give up your power *is* your responsibility. When this happens, each person who gives up control must pay the price for it and suffer the consequences.

I urge each and every reader to make the decision to be responsible for every single thought that passes through your brain and upon which the body acts—even the ones that are programmed into you. The programmers merely use what is already there, enhancing and/or altering it to suit the Illuminati needs.

Get started! Time is wasting! Who is driving your ship??

"Why think thoughts that create unpleasant experiences?"

Mind-Patterns

You have read a lot about mind-patterns throughout this book. I emphasize it constantly because that is what creation and experience are all about.

Thoughts are things. They can actually be measured electro-magnetically by technological devices. When a person is "brain dead," they are disconnected from life support because they are no longer in the body. No thoughts come from the brain, which is a device that the mind uses to interact with physical reality. Even if the entire body is in perfect health, without thought, the person is declared dead.

Since thoughts are concepts and ideas of the soul-personality, we call this the mind-pattern. The mind-pattern is a collection of the thoughts, emotions, and desires of the soul-personality. These are electromagnetic pulses. As they enter or descend into a physical reality, the free-floating atoms and electrons in that reality coalesce around the electromagnetic patterns. These, then, form into protein bases that match the mind-pattern. These protein bases are then the foundation for the DNA which it then creates by combining in various formats. The DNA is the blueprint for the entire body.

Therefore, what you think is what you are—literally. But the thought comes first. If you are unhappy with the way your body looks or acts, go into the mind-pattern that formulated it to change it. This is really a simple process, but only you can do it.

No one can heal you, only you can. No one can change you, only you can. Your own personal mind-pattern created all that you are, and all that is around you.

Your brain is the projection device that beams the patterns out into the frozen energy of physical reality. The atomic structure then reorganizes itself to match the patterns that you emit and imprint upon it. Molecular structures have no mind-pattern of their own. They are like clay that is molded into whatever the artist has in mind. You are an artist.

You can think any thoughts that you want. Why think thoughts that create unpleasant experiences? You can change it instantly. This is up to you. Everything is up to you. Do not blame God-Mind. God-Mind gives you freewill to create within Its existence. This is how God-Mind knows Itself.

Be grateful for all that you have created. It has helped you to "see" inside of yourself. Create nice things. Think happy thoughts!

*"The more you do out of love and respect,
the more you will have with which to work.
This is Universal Law."*

Money:
Wealth & Poverty

Finances are a direct result of the individual's mind-pattern. When you have thoughts of "lack," then you will have less than someone who has thoughts of "abundance." Generally, people who have abandonment issues also have abandonment with money and material things.

Learn a lesson from the Illuminati who want for no material item. They fully believe that they deserve and will have these things, and they do. There is not a doubt or question in their minds. In this sense, they then attract and retain all types of abundance and opulence.

The everyday person should do the same thing. Expecting wealth and prosperity is not arrogant. God-Mind is infinite, and as such, provides for anything that you can imagine. Humans block this by thinking, "I should not have this," or "I do not deserve to have that." This is the result of low self-worth issues that should be released immediately.

Another challenge for people is thinking that you are poor, when in fact you have all the riches in the universe at your disposal. Wealth is not only financial and material, but also emotional and mental as well. When I was really down and out, I one day looked at my little children playing and hugged them tightly. I realized then and there that I had absolutely everything, including hope.

Conversely, I have witnessed fabulously wealthy people who are extremely poor in spirit and in their conduct with their fellow man. They ignore their children and abuse employees in their businesses. They think of themselves as superior to all others, even though they have no idea about God-Mind, or who and what they really are.

Money is a tool to be used for self and others. When you do this unconditionally, but wisely, you receive more and more of it. When you measure it out and keep it restricted, then that is how you will receive and *not* receive it! Use the following affirmations daily:

I now accept and receive all of the abundance, prosperity, and opulence of the Earth plane.

I now receive more money than I can use for myself and others.

Visualize yourself in an endless room filled with every kind of abundance and material thing that you can imagine. Put it and yourself in brown. Then release the image from the mind so that it can go through the necessary universal procedures to manifest physically. Have no doubt! Have no fear! Just *know* that it is so.

When you receive your money and material items, remember to share them with your loved ones, and with anyone truly in need who can benefit from your generosity. This does not mean that you give money to minors to buy alcohol and cigarettes. This does not mean that you give funding to a poor man to buy drugs. Use your funds wisely and freely to allow it to manifest in even greater proportions. The more you do out of love and respect, the more you will have with which to work. This is Universal Law.

Enjoy your wealth! Release your poverty!

*"One day, our reality may be completely
virtual. That will then become
our 'nature.'"*

Nature

Everything is a part of nature, and nature is part of God-Mind. When you think about it, even the chemicals and toxins that are put in food, air, and medications can be broken down to their component parts which start with so-called "natural" items.

Many of the drugs used in hospitals have their origins in the rain forests. It is what mankind does to these products in combining them that is not natural and can lead to harmful effects.

Most of the domestic animals on the Earth are genetically altered so that they manifest in a different way than would be considered part of nature. However, since all things are a projection from the mind-pattern, we must consider then, that everything in existence is part of nature, even if it had a little external help.

There is Mother Nature, human nature, wild by nature, and natural order. All of these are related and are part of each other. Many people feel that they need to be "in nature" to feel good. This means that they want to be outside in a non-technical or artificial environment. Others feel more "natural" sitting in air-conditioning on a synthetic material chair. Both of these sentiments are fine. It is only a question of what makes you feel good for whatever reason.

We must learn to feel comfortable and content no matter what our environment—unless that environment is actually dangerous. Swimming in shark infested waters is dangerous but natural. Breathing asbestos is dangerous but artificial. Neither scenario is good for you.

For those who have allergic reactions, nature can be fatal. The same is true for people with chemical sensitivities. The bottom line is that nature is whatever you want it to be. It all ultimately comes from the same source.

Our true natural state is purely energetic. We exist there simultaneously with the physical. One day, our reality may be completely virtual. That will then become our '"nature."

Always be of a good nature. Treat nature kindly.

"People who leave their shoes all over the place have difficulty in organizing their future and support system."

Neatness

I am compulsively neat. I do this subconsciously to overcome the events from my life that I could not control. By being neat and orderly, I am able to in some way manipulate my surroundings to create an environment to my liking.

Neatness reflects an orderly mind-pattern. Whatever thoughts that you have in your mind are always reflected outward into the world. Look around you. Is there a mess? Is everything in its place? Do you know where every single item is right now?

A messy environment indicates a messy mind. Often, there is an "organized mess." That is not really a mess. Everything is in its place, but you may not know how to find them. The person who controls the "organized mess" knows exactly where everything is. This is an example of a different way of thinking. That person's brain patterns are not usual and do not match with yours.

Sometimes you think something is a mess, but when you stand back far enough, there is a pattern to it. If you are too close to the situation, then you often cannot see the big picture.

In my opinion, things should not only be in their proper places, but they should also look neat. When I am home, I see to it that all things are where they belong when they are not in use. This can be a problem with toys and clothes, and especially shoes and socks. People who leave their shoes all over the place have difficulty in organizing their future and support system.

Some people leave dishes, papers, boxes, and notes all over their countertops. Such individuals have difficulty making choices, communicating, and keeping ideas in perspective.

It is not good to be overly compulsive either. If you have to get up at 3AM because you think there is a speck of lint on a corner of the carpet, this is not right. Such behavior indicates an insecurity about your own mind and thought process. This is also a clue to an abused person who must control and over-compensate everything at all times, or run the risk of losing control and being abused again.

So, be reasonable, but be neat. That goes for your personal hygiene as well. To everything there is a season. Now, that is neat!

"Never tell your parents that you did not
ask to be born. Yes, you did!"

Parents

It is an easy task for anyone with working sexual organs to become a mother or father. It is a bit more difficult to be a parent. Children do not come with a set of instructions, and books written about parenting are usually full of crapola.

In order to be a good parent, you need to look at your own parents, or at least, whoever raised you from childhood. It is very common to have a good relationship with your elderly parents now, but to have had a bad relationship when you all were younger. You must still remember that it is the imprinting from that earlier time period that impacts the way that you are as a parent.

Many people emulate what their parents did to them, or for them, with their own children, mainly because they do not think enough to be different. However, the majority appear to do the exact opposite because they hate their childhood so much. I say, do what is appropriate and right at the moment for your children.

Some parents are abusive to their children. This is because they are victims of this themselves and do not know any better. Intense counseling and release work is in order for all involved in these cases.

As long as your parents are still alive, it is a good idea to tactfully and honestly question them about your childhood. Ask for explanations and clarifications. Many parents will apologize for wrongs done. But even if you do not get an apology, forgive them, because they played a role for you that was necessary for your development as a soul-personality, even if you did not appreciate or understand what was happening at the time. Remember, you chose your parents for a reason. There are no accidents.

If your parents keep putting you down and criticizing you, let them know how you feel about that, nicely. If it is difficult for you to verbalize it, then send an email or a regular letter with your feelings. If your parents are no longer on the Earth plane, go through the Oversoul to communicate with them. No matter how you do it, do not let the opportunity pass you by.

If there is still no change, then minimize your interactions with them, but still keep in contact. You will find that if you release these memories and childhood feelings, you will "grow up the inner child." Otherwise, every time you are with your parents or people who reflect them, you will revert to acting like the "little child within," and your experiences will be painful and inappropriate. This is especially true when dealing with a mate or spouse. We tend to marry people like our parents because we have not worked out our issues and need to recreate them with others so that we can work through these parental issues.

You will see that when the little child inside of you becomes an adult, then all of your interactions with others is based on an adult understanding of the situations instead of the childlike, emotional reactions. Outcomes and life experiences become easier and more pleasant.

Never tell your parents that you did not ask to be born. Yes, you did! You chose them for the necessary learning that they provide. No one said that you had to like or enjoy the experience. The strongest medicines have the most horrible tastes.

Every time you have to punish a child or interact with your child in any way, first ask yourself if this is what your parents did to you and how did you feel about it. Ask yourself how you would have wanted them to act or what you would have wanted to hear from them. Then, ask which way or what new way is most appropriate for the current situation. Yes, it may take a bit of thinking, but you will save your child from years of therapy later on.

"Honor thy Father and Mother," so the Bible says. Perhaps we should add the need to understand them, too. They were the mechanisms for us to be here. That is valuable.

*"Be kind to your pets. You never know
when you will become one."*

Pets

Everyone should have the experience of having a pet at least once in their lives. Pets teach us unconditional love and patience. They do not care who we are or anything about our past. They only care that we love and take care of them.

Some people use pets as friends. They cannot get along with other people too well, so they use the animal kingdoms as their companions. After all, a cat or dog will not talk back to you, or tell you that your opinions are incorrect.

There are many individuals, especially women, who substitute pets for children. If the woman never had a child and feels a void in her life, it is likely that she will get one or more cats that she cares for as if they were her children. Although this would seem sad at the surface, it is wonderful that such a choice exists. I would hope that at some point in life, the woman would perhaps think of becoming a single parent and adopt a child, even of another race. If this is not feasible, then a pet is a fine substitute.

In a matter of speaking, we are all pets of the Illuminati. They consider us to be weak and small-minded animals who are not able to care for ourselves. So, they have taken it upon themselves to be our Lords and Masters. How benevolent of them!

Pets are part of an animal species group mind, much like a hive mentality. When a specific animal or pet has spent a lot of time with its owner or master, it may become "humanized." This means that it learned a range of intelligence and emotions from human contact and interaction that brought it way beyond the normal capacities of its species.

Then, after its physical death, it may join with other members of its species with similar experience and understanding, to enter into a human body for the first time and become a rudimentary human soul-personality. Usually, such a human is handicapped both physically and mentally. This enables both the human and its caretakers to learn unconditional love.

Be kind to your pets. You never know when you will become one.

*"Be careful for what you thankfully pray,
you **will** receive it! "*

Prayer

There is a lot of misunderstanding about this function. Most of
society only knows what their religions have taught them. God-
Mind does not have set times or dates in which to receive prayer
from creation. Prayer is acceptable at all times, in any language
because ultimately, it converts to hyperspace language.

Prayer is a function of left-brain. This is the logistical side of the
brain, and the home of the ego. This is where lack is perceived,
or the idea that "I have not." Therefore, it sends out a message
that "it needs."

The left-brain thinks that it is separate from the God-Mind within.
This is really a form of insanity. You cannot be apart from the
very substance of which you are created. Therefore, the mere act
of thinking is a form of prayer because it sends out a request or
idea that can be brought into fruition.

The proper way to pray is to thank the God-Mind for already
providing you with everything that you need, want, or desire. It
is already accomplished. In the Eternal Now, everything has
already happened. That is why you pray to thank for already
having received, even though in physical reality you may not
have caught up with it yet. But, whatever you pray for is
already there.

Sometimes you pray for something that is not good for you. Your Oversoul may divert the energy to something more appropriate. Then you think that God has not heard you or that the answer to your prayer was "no." However, this is not the case. God-Mind always hears you because It *is* you. You are made up of It.

Very often, the object of your desires may not come into physicality until you are ready to receive it, even if you want it *now!* You must be patient and know that all things happen when they are supposed to happen. This is how we learn to align our freewill with God's will. They are really the same thing, but our ego portion has its own timetable.

Purple color is the energy of prayer. Surround yourself in it when you give prayers of thanks. Whenever we pray, we are really going through the connection of our Oversoul. This has a silver color. God-Mind has a gold color. White is the God-Mind liaison with all parts of Itself.

Be careful for what you thankfully pray—you *will* receive it!

*"Know that you are always under Divine
Protection. "*

Protection

There are no safe places, only safe people. Protection is a state of mind, like everything else. If you have an absolute knowing that you are part of God-Mind and everything in existence is part of God-Mind, how can you be harmed? Such a thought is insanity. God-Mind does not harm Itself.

For those of you who are not yet secure in your knowing, there are visualizations that can be done to enhance the protection that you feel. Many of these methods are outlined in my *Healer's Handbook: A Journey Into Hyperspace (Sky Books, 1999)*. These protection methods involve the use of the color "violet" which acts as a filtering and protection energy.

Visualizing mirrors placed around yourself and facing away from you deflects negativity coming toward you. Never surround yourself in white light because this washes away all other chakra colors and depletes you.

There are positions of the arms and legs, as well as affirmations that you can employ to enhance protection around yourself.

However, we must all look at the mind-patterns that make us feel unprotected and vulnerable. This is a form of insecurity that comes from low self-worth issues and that famous victimization mentality I continually yell about.

When you feel like a target and victim, you will attract a perpetrator of one degree or another. No matter what alarm systems you use or how high your perimeter fence, there will be one or more ways to break through these barriers to reach you and/or your possessions.

Protection is unnecessary when you realize that you are always safe and secure within God-Mind, no matter what is going on around you. You are part of God-Mind and therefore can never be destroyed. Danger is an illusion of victimization. Any attack, injury, or theft is created by you to realize that it is all a reflection of your own mind and you cannot lose any part of yourself.

Rejection is God's protection. What you do not get is okay. Know that you are always under Divine Protection.

"Religion is designed for those with limited thinking capacity who are afraid or unwilling to know more."

Religion

Religion is said to be the opiate of the people. This means that the masses use their faith and belief system to fall back upon when they do not understand their own lives. It also means that the people use religion to ignore reality and blindly accept what they are told by religious leaders and doctrines in the same way that one would accept a drug-induced stupor.

All religions, no matter what the premise, are a form of mind-control. Religion is a way for a small group of people to control large masses of people through fear, intimidation, and blind following. There is absolutely no self-interpretation. You must believe what you are told about God and the world. Any deviation is blasphemous.

Here is some news—God-Mind does *not* have a religion! God-Mind is *** All That Is.*** It has no agenda, no punishment, no doctrine, no demands, and no ritual. All of that comes from people who want to control others.

God-Mind is neutral and allows all things so that It can know Itself. It cannot narrow Self down to rules and regulations, and throw lightning bolts at those who do not believe. It allows freewill, the direct opposite of what religion dictates.

Admittedly, many devoutly religious people live a good life never having to explain anything since all is "God's Will." But, they never learn truth. They never understand life. They know *nothing* of God. It is all a mystery to them.

Life should not be a mystery. Religion precludes personal responsibility and promotes ignorance. No religion has all the answers, but each of you does inside of yourselves. Look there. Ritual and ceremony are symbolic, and in actuality are meaningless. Religion is designed for those with limited thinking capacity who are afraid or unwilling to know more.

A New World Religion will be imposed upon the Earth. It will encompass all that has gone before, taking the best of deception and mind-control, and putting it into a neat little package that *all* will be forced to obey. Not a pretty picture. But then, no religion ever is. It has been the source of war and hate since time began.

*"You are the writer, director, and
producer of your life."*

Responsibility

The bottom line of everything is that you are each responsible for totally everything in your life no matter what it is. Case closed!

This means that you are *never* to blame anyone or anything else for your particular circumstances. This even goes for how you perceive the world globally.

Let us go back to the mind-pattern. What you think and feel is projected out into the Earth plane, and reflected back for you on every level. This is what happens when a soul-personality does not take responsibility for its own thinking. God-Mind does not intervene. It stays neutral and allows all things to occur, no matter how human beings judge them.

If you do not like the "movie" that is playing around you, then change the film, which is your mind-pattern. Yes, there are external forces that we use as tools to accomplish the situations and experiences. But we attract these by our mind-patterns. Thoughts are electromagnetic and attract molecular structure that then arranges itself into the patterns that we project out. So perhaps the trees release pollen at a certain time of the year, which reflects species mind-patterns, but you as an individual attract a reaction to the pollen because of the way you think—in this case, in an irritable manner.

Take stock of your life. Make a list of what you do not like about yourself. You will see that this matches what you do not like about other people, places, and things. Therefore, if you correct the way you think, all of these people, places, and things will no longer bother you.

If you collect debt, plan to pay it off. No one forced you to buy anything. That was your choice. Do not curse the credit card companies, the banks, or even the collection agencies. They *all* reflect you and play a role in your life that you have created for yourself.

If you are unhappy with your job or marriage, do not blame your boss or spouse. Just ask yourself, what does this relationship and/ or work circumstance reflect for me? What is this motivating me to change within myself? Bless all those who play a role for you. You are the writer, director, and producer of your life. You are a production company by yourself.

Take responsibility!!

*"It is best to remain with one partner to
maintain balance and peace."*

Sex

There is not a more thought about topic in all the universes! It is said that men think about sex every few seconds. I think women do the same, except that they do not want to admit it.

Why all of the fuss about sex? There are a couple of reasons. The main, inherent reason is because biologically, it is the only natural way to procreate the species. There are more women then men so that one male can theoretically impregnate more than one woman and produce more children to continue the species. One sperm fertilizes one egg. A male produces enough sperm in one ejaculate to populate the entire planet. Females have limited eggs with which they are born. A male can have children all of his adult life. Female reproductive years are limited. This is an example of how God-Mind manifests in physical reality.

Father God is infinite and always productive. Mother Earth is finite and limited in fertility. As above, so below. This is where sex comes in.

Since humanity is split into male and female components, the natural desire is to merge this into the One. This represents humans attempting to return to the God-Mind source. The sensation of orgasm is related to the release of creative energy by the God-Mind. In effect, sexual activity is a poor replica of the creative actions of God-Mind.

Many religions teach that sexual relations should be for procreation only. They discourage wasting or "spilling" seed. This was a form of population control and was designed to increase the numbers of people. God-Mind has no such rules on sex, except that without the emotion behind it, it feels empty. That is the difference between having sex and making love.

A male projects out his entire energy, including his DNA, when he has an orgasm. A female intakes this and is imprinted by what the male projects. Therefore, if a woman is promiscuous and has many partners, she can become both physically and mentally ill, because she is constantly imprinting different patterns on her field. You will never see a healthy prostitute! Males do not get imprinted by females. That is why it is so easy for them to leave a relationship without all the emotional suffering that females go through.

When two males have sex, their energies amplify each other because they are both projecting out and multiplying energies. This is why homosexual males feel boosted by their sexual activities and seek more. It is like being on drugs. Two females having sex receive no energy from each other and may feel unfulfilled in their relationships.

The expression of love between two people ultimately results in a sexual union because the need to merge and symbolize the God-Mind is a natural outgrowth of unconditional love. Even close friends of the same sex will sometimes find sexual feelings toward each other, even though they may not talk about or act upon it.

Pornography is designed by the Illuminati controllers to open up the lower chakra system so that control of the mind can be accomplished. We know from programming experiments that when a person is brought to near orgasmic levels, information and imprinting can be entered or extracted from the mind. The person is left vulnerable and impressionable. When sex is brought to the surface, the targeted person will do just about anything. This is the thrust behind marketing and advertisements, as well as governmental broadcasts. Subliminal sexual carrier waves are sent via television, radio, and computer signals.

Masturbation is the soul-personality's attempt to love itself, balance itself, and redistribute pent-up energies. Abstaining from sexual activity for a while actually increases psychic abilities as the two energies are related and dependent on one another. If you are overactive sexually, your psychic abilities are weakened. However, they both go hand-in-hand. After a strong psychic experience or act, sexuality is needed to close off the person energetically. Vice versa, after frequent sexual activity, abstinence is necessary to build up the psychic energy.

It is best to remain with one partner to maintain balance and peace. It is best to truly love that partner. It is best to make love, rather than just have sex. A baby born of love is a wonderful gift.

"It is better to be alone than to wish you were alone. Select, rather than settle."

Spouses

As a popular song says, "This could be heaven or this could be hell!" Most world cultures dictate that a person should marry and have a family. If you do not, then something is "wrong" with you. Maybe you are gay. Well, gays have spouses, too.

We should always remember that everything that you ever need is inside of you. You need no one and no thing to complete yourself. You are already complete in the God-Mind. It is your choice to share with whomever you so choose. It is not mandatory that you have a life partner. Some people are much better off living by themselves and having an occasional fling or relationship. This is fine as long as both individuals know that this is all that is intended.

When you decide to marry someone, the absolute only reason should be unconditional love. Marriage should have nothing to do with money, status, business, or any other physical reason. Nor should it have to do with race or religion. God-Mind shows Its face in great diversified ways.

You should be faithful to your spouse unless **both** of you agree to do otherwise. If you do stray, do not say anything as it will devastate the other person. Just **do not** do it again! If you feel

109

the need to cheat on your spouse, you must ask yourself why. Most of the time it is because you feel inadequate or unwanted, and need to prove to yourself that you are still desirable. Always try counseling with a decent therapist before you decide to go your separate ways.

Sometimes, two people decide to have a marriage of convenience, whether financial, emotional, or otherwise. As long as both parties agree to this status, it is okay. Never stay together for the children's sake. They know and feel the tension and unhappiness, and then you teach them wrong ideas about relationships.

Many people are concerned about finding their life mate or soulmate. There is a difference between soulmates, twin souls, and twin flames. It is a matter of degree. Soulmates can be good friends or "travel" partners during many incarnations. They can have the same Oversoul. Twin souls are of the same Oversoul, and of the same root soul-personality that has split at some point and always are reciprocals of one another. Twin flames are basically the same person in two bodies of different sex. They always feel compelled to be together. Sometimes, they have a love/hate relationship because they are so much alike.

It is better to be alone than to wish you were alone. Select, rather than settle. Never choose to marry someone who is like your parent. Never marry hoping to change anyone. Do not be like a parent to your spouse. Have a long and happy life together!

*"**Now** is **your** time!"*

Time

There is no such thing as time. Time is an illusion of a linear physical reality. In actuality, time and space do not exist. To the God-Mind or All That Is, all events and thoughts occur simultaneously. Therefore, there is no past, present, or future, only the Eternal Now.

With this concept comes the realization that in eternity, all things are possible because there is the "time" to create everything. This means that no matter what you think, it will come into being at some point in existence.

This leads me to a discussion on alternate timelines, sometimes called parallel realities. Since within the God-Mind all things are possible and all things come into being, there must be various, even infinite versions of everything in existence. Every possibility is explored in the God-Mind. This is how It knows Itself.

This also means that there are many versions of each of us in different realities. In effect, there is all the time in existence to accomplish what we need to learn and do. Nothing is impossible.

Time is considered either a friend or an enemy by most people. But if it is not real, how can it have such a powerful influence on our lives? It is from the conditioned belief that time is a force that we can use in our lives for our benefit. Time is kind of like money—we can use our time wisely, or waste it.

The fact is, we must use the illusion of time the way we see fit, no matter what anyone thinks of our timetable. If you want to sit around the house all day and do nothing, or work three jobs and paint the house, it is *all okay*! Eventually, you will feel the motivation from your inner clock to change your perception of time as it applies to your lifestyle.

Your mind-pattern determines what you perceive and use as time. Reptilians understand that they have all the time in existence to accomplish their goals. Humans feel rushed all the time. Aging, or the belief in aging, is a factor. When you know that you actually have Eternal Life, then you can put your "time" into proper perspective.

Live life to the fullest that you can. Do whatever you can all of the time. *Now* is *your* time! Have a *good* time!!

*"With tolerance, comes the uplifting
of the mind-pattern."*

Tolerance

The word "tolerance" has many connotations. Many people think of race relations when this word pops up. However, there is much more to "tolerance" than that.

We need to have tolerance for ourselves, our loved ones, and especially the people with whom we live. Tolerance requires the attributes of patience, understanding, letting go, and consistency. This means that you are able to deal with a person, place, or thing easily and without stress. Tolerance does not require unconditional love, or even liking someone or something.

I can tolerate you, but hate your guts! I can tolerate hot, humid weather, but despise it and wish for winter. I can tolerate a job I dislike while patiently looking for another one.

To be tolerant, you must learn how to center yourself, balance your energy, and release the object of your discontent. This takes practice, experience, and a desire to do so. Keep in mind again, that if you cannot tolerate someone or something, you must ask yourself what is being reflected for you from within your own mind-pattern. This is key.

I, for example, find it difficult to tolerate annoying people. Of course, I am referring to people that I in particular find to be annoying. This means that there is something about them that resonates within my own mind constructs. I find myself to be annoying, and then see this in a person who plays the role for me. Or, I may know that others find me to be annoying at times, so I look for this in people I meet so that I can see this in front of me. In this way, I may develop methods to eliminate that energy in me or convert it to something more tolerable for myself and others.

It helps to actually write a list of what you find to be intolerable. Take your time. No one has to see it. Work on each of the issues as needed. Perceive these items on your list as being part of who you are at the moment. See this in action in your daily life. As soon as you catch yourself being this way, stop, center, take a deep breath, and then consciously correct the issue. You may have to force it at first, but with practice and proficiency, it will become second nature. Work through the entire list in this fashion.

Before long, you will suddenly realize that you are able to tolerate anything. You do not have to like it, but it becomes tolerable. With tolerance, comes the uplifting of the mind-pattern. We will all be better people for it, and the world will be more tolerant and tolerable. How wonderful!

"Soon there will be teleportation devices available to the public."

Travel

Travel is a topic that I know a lot about! I travel almost 90% of my time. We can talk about many different forms of travel and I will touch briefly on each of these.

Most of you reading this will be doing physical travel in your life; getting from Point A to Point B. Here are a few suggestions that I have for you in light of today's volatile world situations:

> • *Always travel light. You can wash clothing when you get there. It is better to take one carry-on bag than wait at an airport carousel hoping that your bag arrives with you.*

> • *Make sure that you have valid photo identification with you, and more than one type, i.e., a passport as well as driver's license.*

> • *Have plenty of local currency on you and one valid credit card. Most places accept American dollars, but in certain "snobby" countries they will not accept it.*

> • *Always look well-dressed, but not flashy. Groom well before starting your trip.*

• *Do not argue with security people or immigration officials.*

• *Keep a calm demeanor and wear cologne or perfume.*

• *Make sure you know your route, airline, train, or bus company, flight numbers and times, contact names, hotel addresses, etc.*

• *Keep a list of important phone numbers with you at all times.*

• *Make sure that someone at home knows your itinerary at all times.*

• *Call or email someone at home often.*

• *Keep any medications, vitamins, herbs, and elixirs in a shoulder bag or fanny pack with you at all times.*

• *Have a loaded camera available for opportune moments.*

• *Use protection techniques around you and your vehicle constantly. Thank God for delivering you safely to each destination.*

• *Be selective and extremely careful of the food you eat. Drink only bottled water in strange locations, preferably distilled.*

• *Check all beds, bathrooms, and walking areas for bugs, insects, small animals, and debris.*

• *Check weather reports and local news daily.*

• *Always have an alternate plan in all circumstances.*

If you are doing astral (which I do not recommend) or hyperspace travel, you only need to remember the following:

• *Always use protection techniques around yourself before beginning.*

• *Keep your T-Bar archetype balanced before, during, and after each trip.*

• *Make sure that your body is in a safe and comfortable place.*

• *Go to brown after each "travel" session.*

"Everyone and everything has truth in it."

Truth

The truth is that there is only one truth—the absolute truth. Not the relative truth, or the near truth, or a possible truth. Only the absolute truth.

There have been many who say that what is true for one person may not be true for another. If something is not true all of the time and in every circumstance, then it is not true...period.

Personal truths are always true for that individual. If there was something that "used to be true" but is not anymore, than it never was true. Truth stands alone and cannot be changed by time or space.

In Hebrew, a truly hyperspace language before modern corruptions, the English transliteration for "truth" is "Ehmaat." When you remove the first syllable (vowel), you get "Maat," the root word for death. The symbolism here is that if you take away from the truth even one vowel, you receive death. Something to remember.

Using color codes from the Language of Hyperspace, pale orange helps us to see the truth. If you put someone in pale orange while they speak, and they lie to you, the color will change.

If they are telling the truth, the pale orange will remain. If you force the pale orange around them, and they want to lie or deceive you, they will not be able to speak. You can also use this on newspapers and books.

This is why pale orange is the color of the sacral chakra. This section of the body is related to creativity and productivity. These must come from a place of truth in order to be of value.

You must be true to yourself as well. If you fool yourself, you will also fool others. Self-deception makes you a deceptive person. It is said that the truth hurts. Not really. Truth itself is harmless and can never hurt. It is the realization that we have lied to ourselves that hurts.

One of the ten aspects of God-Mind is Truth. Therefore, it is also part of our composition. Everyone and everything has truth in it. Let us begin to use it daily in every application of our lives. Live in Truth.

*"Our world is ringed with detection
devices and weapons that ensure total
control of our skies and beyond."*

UFOs

There is not a more misunderstood topic in existence than UFOs! There are many things which can be categorized as an unidentified flying object. Such things have been seen since time began. I will attempt to put this topic into perspective.

In ancient times there were indeed beings who came here from other worlds within our own universe. There were also entities which visited here from other realities, sometimes called "alternate" or "parallel" universes. There are even vehicles from other time periods within our own timeline. To say the least, our planet is quite a hot spot. This is because of its unique position on the edge of one of the spirals in our pinwheel-shaped galaxy. It is also because of its interdimensional position on the edge of physical reality and hyperspace. This planet is the O'Hare Airport of the universe!

Many descriptions of ancient space travelers and aliens are depicted on cave walls, Medieval church murals, paintings, and even in Bible stories. Hollywood science-fiction is filled with them.

The truth is that since the last quarter of the 20th century, almost all modern UFO sightings have been of craft made and operated from the planet Earth!

True, many of these crafts were based on alien technology to begin with, but these days all of them seen operating within our atmosphere are under Earth control. Very often they masquerade as aliens to fool the public and deny culpability.

Since the last half of the 20th century, the powers that control this world have seen to it that no true aliens get too close to the planet. Our world is ringed with detection devices and weapons that ensure total control of our skies and beyond.

The fact is that since the 1950s, both the Moon and Mars have been under Earth-based domination and manipulation. There is steady and regular transportation between the Earth and other parts of this galaxy by humans flying vehicles that the ancient Indians referred to as Vimanas—craft that fly into space and never crash. Ancient East Indian texts talk explicitly about the building and operation of such craft down to the nuts and bolts, so to speak.

UFOs have intrigued the population for decades since the first publicized sighting of nine UFOs near Mt. Rainier in Washington State in 1947. This was followed shortly that same year by the infamous flying saucer crashes outside of a ranch in Roswell, New Mexico, and also in Aztec, New Mexico. Much of the current UFO technology came from those two incidents. The procedure for building these crafts for humans was called "reverse engineering."

Much of the building and testing of these vehicles takes place in secret bases all over the world. Many of these places have become "holy sites" in UFO lore, and are constantly sought after by UFO buffs and enthusiasts.

In the future, these vehicles will become standard equipment to the public. Shows like *Star Trek, X-Files, Star Wars*, etc., are all designed to imprint these modes of travel onto the psyche of the public so that when they are brought into the open, there will be no surprises, only complete acceptance.

Also to be released is the technology that goes along with the UFO mindset such as Stargates, wormholes, transporters, molecular synthesizers, and laser weapons. These devices already exist in private government/scientific research use.

There are UFOs from other dimensional spaces or realities that "bleep" in from time to time. The rulers of this planet cannot easily control their comings and goings. We will continue to see those objects. At least some of this will still remain a mystery for the time being.

*"Choose carefully what you project out.
Somewhere, in some reality, it will
take hold."*

Visualizations

Visualization is a beautiful part of your brain and mind. This function is physically located at the pineal gland at the center of the head. Visualization pulls the creativity of the right-brain and the logic of the left-brain together to create and manifest something that you have imaged and projected out.

I have enumerated many techniques on visualization in my books and videos, especially my *Healer's Handbook: A Journey Into Hyperspace* (Sky Books, 1999). Anything that you wish to create is already accomplished in hyperspace and God-Mind.

Some people have told me that they cannot visualize or see colors and shapes. I tell them that if they can daydream, they can visualize. Daydreaming is a fantasy or wish in the mind that you play out as a mental movie. If you use the right color codes, then that movie or image can be brought into the Earth plane. All you have to do is send the perfected mental image in brown up to your Oversoul, then put yourself in brown.

The color brown says to the image in hyperspace, "happen now." Brown's meaning is grounding in the present moment. Always remember to end each visualization that way if you want it to occur now.

Whenever you do your visualization work, use visual aids if necessary. Whatever you need to look at to perfect the image is acceptable. Once you have the image as perfectly as you can imagine it, let it go and do not go back to it. Let the energy go on its way to achieve the image. Constantly redoing the work or checking on it disrupts the energy flow and stops the visualization from reaching fruition.

When you do healing work, this is a visualization. It does not matter if you simply see the patient as well, or if you use actual techniques that lead to wellness; all of it is visualization.

Some teachers have used different names and terms like creative imaging, guided meditation, walk-throughs, etc. They are all the same thing. Whenever you create into the physical world, you are visualizing.

Choose carefully what you project out. Somewhere, in some reality, it will take hold. Most likely it will manifest within the context of your own Oversoul matrix. You are responsible for every image that you think. Thoughts are things. Thoughts become things. Remember this!

"Water is a flush and hydrator, not a food.
It should be neutral and inert."

Water

Our bodies are over 80% water. Our planet is almost 70% water. See a trend here? Water is very important and mandatory for life to exist. Water is also a symbolism in our dreams that represents the flow of life or the ocean of life.

There have been many "scientific" studies done about water and how much you need. I have heard everything from "water is dangerous and toxic to the human body and should not ever be taken," to "everyone needs 8 to 10 or more glasses per day." All of these are wrong.

The human body was designed to drink distilled water. Ancient humans used to drink rain water, which is naturally distilled by the atmosphere and water cycles of the Earth. However, in modern times, rain water is polluted and contaminated and should never be ingested.

"New Agers" and some scientists say that distilled water pulls nutrients from your body and hurts you. This is not correct. Distilled water takes toxins out and pulls residues from all body systems.

Water is a flush and hydrator, not a food. It should be neutral and inert. You get vitamins and minerals from food that you eat and supplements that you take, not from water. Drinking too much water causes over-hydration, literally drowning the body. Over-hydration keeps fluids in the cell structure of your body, preventing nutrients and oxygen from passing through. Dehydration is also dangerous and causes the body systems to fail from lack of fluid flows.

The amount of water that you should drink depends upon your body configuration. If you are a 400 pound Sumo wrestler, then you might need ten glasses per day. If you are a five foot tall, thin woman, you only need about four glasses. Heat, humidity, and exercise intensity require adjustments to daily intakes.

Spring water often contains a high radon and toxic mineral content. Tap water contains chlorine, fluorides, and other toxins. Do not drink these types of water. Do not drink water from volcanic areas as that contains extremely high sulfur and radon. Do not drink your own urine—besides being really disgusting, your body passed it out because it is full of waste!

"So, never complain about the weather. You are the one pressing all the buttons and turning the dials."

Weather

So what can you do about the weather? First, you need to know what it really is, then you can see how simple it is to actually do something about it!

The weather in any area is a direct result and manifestation of the mind-patterns and emotions of the people who live in that area. This is what attracts people to a given location to live or vacation.

For example, if you live in the desert, it implies that you feel barren and empty inside yourself. It also means that you could have a "hot" temper and a "dry" sense of humor.

Those who live in arctic or extreme cold climates are generally "cold" emotionally and sensually. It is hard for them to empathize with others or feel anything at all. These people are desensitized to experience the "same old, same old."

The same applies to the geology of an area. In volcanic regions, the population tends to be very steady and even with emotions until one day, they just blow up! These people bottle up their feelings until they just cannot hold them in any more.

Similarly, people in areas prone to earthquakes need a jolt in their lives every so often because they just do not pay attention to the important things in life. They do not realize what they have until it is gone.

Populations in tornado areas are in need of seeing other realities and "spinning" their ideas and emotions differently. That is why tornadoes are "selective" in where they hit. Each individual, as well as the collective in the area, attracts the weather conditions that match the emotions and thoughts of those living there.

If global weather changes, i.e., global warming, then the implication is that humanity as a species is heating up the way they feel and think. All the volatile emotions are coming to the surface. The weather responds by heating up the planet and making storms more potent. This matches the global society conditions.

The good news is that once this is accomplished, the weather should go back to more "normalized" standards. Of course, this does not take into account external factors like the HAARP Project and other weather manipulations by the government. But even those manipulations reflect humanity as a whole.

Floods represent those who feel overwhelmed by life and are inundated with worry and concern that wash them away from their daily life. The key to all of this is balance and centering, and doing release work constantly.

Gray clouds are a sign of doubt and confusion with some aspect of life. Wind means change is coming and you must prepare for it. Blue skies are a sure sign that your communication with the God-Mind within is in good order. Snow can be cleansing and purity, while a severe blizzard is being bogged down by the process of elimination of anger that leaves you cold and buried in unemotion. Rain is also cleansing, but on a more current daily level that might make you feel depressed or confused about what you are releasing.

So, never complain about the weather. You are the one pressing all the buttons and turning the dials. As they say in the Great Lakes area, "if you don't like the weather….wait five minutes!"

*"Ultimately, it is the image that you hold
mentally of yourself and the related
emotions and mind-patterns that
determine your weight."*

Weight

This is a "weighty" issue for most. Diets do not work because
your body configuration is in direct correlation to the mind-
pattern. This is very simple – it does not matter what you eat.

When you have a need for insulation from the outside world, you
gain weight. When you need to put up a barrier between you and
everyone else, you become heavyset. The weight becomes a fence
or security system. You can eat crackers and drink water all day,
and you will remain fat. If you have no insulating mind-pattern,
then you can eat hot fudge sundaes all day and be thin as a rail.
Notice this among the people that you already know.

Women who are grotesquely overweight usually have had some
type of sexual abuse in their earlier life. The weight is to make
them unattractive, and in this way they protect themselves from
further abuse. This is the same for men, but the abuse tends to be
more emotional than physical with males.

Whenever you eat or drink anything, first mentally flush the food
with violet color for at least 33 seconds. Then, mentally direct
the atomic structure of the food and drink to do for your body
and mind whatever you want it to do, i.e., grow muscles, thicken
your hair, improve digestion, etc. Otherwise, the natural

intelligence of the body's cells store a lot of it for fat in case of times of starvation or famine. This is genetically programmed into you.

Of course, exercise and supplements are important in the world in which we live. But, ultimately, it is the image that you hold mentally of yourself and the related emotions and mind-patterns that determine your weight. Weight is subjective anyway. On the moon you would hardly weigh anything, yet, you might look overweight. So, do not go by the numbers on the scale, go by how you look, how you feel, and what you want for yourself.

Keep the following affirmation firmly in your mind every day:

I am now at my most perfect body weight and shape.

Think it constantly and it will become the truth for you. It is the truth for you right now anyway, since you reflect the most perfect match for your current mind-patterns.

Think perfectly. You are a reflection of God-Mind. Always remember that!

"When something fits your frequency, it is successful, always."

Work

Most people cringe at the word! No one wants to get up every day of the week and go to work. There is traffic and weather to contend with on the way and coming home. While you are there, you have to devote yourself to making other people wealthy. All you get is a salary, limited benefits, a small vacation, lots of aggravation, and, if you have a good year, perhaps a bonus.

Most of the work forces in developed countries are not happy with what they do. A majority work only to pay off debt, survive on a daily basis, or use their job as a stepping stone to something else.

At the end of your life, do you want to be happy about what you have done at work, or do you want to regret that you have wasted your life?

The best advice that you can give to anyone is to work at what you truly love to be doing, even if that work does not make you rich. When you wake up every morning excited about going to work and looking forward to your daily activities, then you will be better at what you do, have a healthier body, and that leads to an improved mind-pattern that provides you with abundance and security.

If you are a student, start by planning your education to accommodate the work that you love. Do not be talked into studying subjects that lead to an unhappy profession. If you want to be a gymnast, but your parents want you to be an accountant, be a gymnast! If you think that you want to be a doctor or lawyer because you will make more money, but your talents are in cooking, you will be an unhappy, unfilled lawyer or doctor who loves to cook. There are no winners in that scenario.

If you are in a situation where you cannot find work, look at your mind-pattern. Is it self-sabotage going on, or are you looking for a job that does not fit you?

Always consider making your own work. This can range from anything from childcare to selling handicrafts, or even writing stories. Think of what you love and do best. Everyone has something with which they are talented and love to do. ***That*** is your work. You can start your real work part-time while you work your main job. Eventually, the "love work" will take over. Do not give up because of setbacks, rejection, or financial worries. When something fits your frequency, it is successful, always.

Now, get to work!